HiDiNG DeaD BODieS

YOUR NO-NONSENSE PATH TO SEARCH ENGINE OPTIMISATION (SEO) GLORY

"THE BEST PLACE TO HIDE A DEAD BODY IS PAGE TWO OF GOOGLE"
- THE HUFFINGTON POST

GAVIN DUFF

DEDICATION

For my son Caden, of course. The bravest and strongest human being I've ever known.

CONTENTS

INTRODUCTION

Welcome.

Are you in the mood for an in-depth exploration into the art and science of Search Engine Optimisation (SEO)?

Not many people are. I get that. But I promise you it'll be interesting.

The title of this book, "Hiding Dead Bodies," might seem a bit macabre at first glance, but it draws from a well-known quip in the world of digital marketing: *"The best place to hide a dead body is page two of Google."* This saying humorously underscores a fundamental truth about search engine behaviour - users rarely venture beyond the first page of search results. In fact, studies have shown that the vast majority of clicks go to the top listings on page one, rendering page two practically invisible. Thus, being relegated to the second page (or beyond) effectively means your content is hidden from the audience you're trying to reach.

In my career, I have actually utilised this concept in rather unconventional ways. There have been instances where known brands have sought my expertise to ensure certain content did not gain prominence in search results, particularly in high ranking negative news stories or old website pages. Reverse PR, if you will. While these scenarios were rare, they highlight the nuanced control that effective SEO practices can exert over digital visibility. However, this book is about the opposite approach - ensuring that your content is not hidden but prominently displayed, capturing the attention it deserves. If the title led you to expect a guide on obscuring your digital footprint, I must apologise for the misdirection. Our focus here is firmly on mastering the art of being seen and heard in the crowded digital landscape. I *will* cover both though. Also, in that case, you should have read the back of the book.

This book is primarily crafted from the ground up to serve as your guide in the ever-evolving field of digital marketing, specifically through the lens of SEO. For many years, I've dedicated my career to navigating the shifting landscapes of digital marketing, carving out successful strategies across various platforms and industries. With a wealth of experience under my belt, I bring to you a distilled essence of what effective SEO really entails.

SEO crosses over into so many other areas and it's not possible to cover it all, so I have focused on what truly matters. That's because this book emerges from a need to clarify, educate, and lead in an industry riddled with misconceptions and fleeting trends. It's written to cut through the noise and offer a clear, comprehensive understanding of SEO as it stands today and as it is likely to evolve in the foreseeable future. Unlike many resources, this book does not rely on visuals or illustrations to make its point—these are readily available online, and anyone can access them with a simple Google search. Instead, I focus purely on conveying through my words the depth of knowledge gained through extensive professional practice. I'll focus on what works and I'll ignore what doesn't. That, or I'll debunk the latter.

In the realm of SEO, simplicity often collides with the technical and creative demands of the field. While I strive to maintain clarity and accessibility throughout the text, there will be instances where we delve into more complex ideas—always with the intention of providing you with a thorough understanding that benefits your SEO endeavours.

Throughout this book, I tackle not only the foundational concepts that underpin SEO but also the nuanced strategies that can significantly enhance the visibility and effectiveness of online content. This is not a book of fluff or unfounded claims—it is fairly serious, intended to elevate the practice of SEO among professionals and enthusiasts alike.

In writing this book, one of my primary goals is to also dispel the myriad myths that surround SEO. Too many times, these myths lead even the most earnest marketer astray. I address these misconceptions head-on, providing reasoned explanations and evidence-based practices that replace folklore with strategy.

Another significant motive for this is to distinguish genuine SEO expertise from the pretence often encountered in the digital marketing sphere. The market is saturated with individuals and agencies that claim SEO proficiency; however, genuine expertise - as demonstrated through sustained success and innovation - is rare. This book is for those who aspire to rise above the mediocre, equipping themselves with knowledge and skills that are both comprehensive and adaptable.

My extensive background in digital marketing over two decades, where I have orchestrated campaigns for everything from startups to major international brands, gives me a panoramic view of how SEO fits within broader marketing objectives. Each chapter of this book is a result of real-world experience, blending theoretical knowledge with practical applications to provide insights not only into 'how' but also 'why' certain SEO practices are effective.

I'll also embrace the intersection of SEO with fields like User Experience (UX), neuromarketing, and cyberpsychology, exploring how human behaviour and technological interaction impact search engine visibility and content engagement. These insights help refine tactics that go beyond ridiculous and pointless attempts at algorithm manipulation, focusing instead on creating genuine engagement and value.

As we venture through the concepts and strategies within this book, remember that the ultimate goal of SEO is to connect and communicate effectively with your target audience. It's about ensuring that the right people find the right information at the right time. With this book, I invite you to elevate your understanding of SEO, dispel the myths that might have clouded your efforts, and achieve a level of mastery that sets you apart in the digital marketing realm.

Let us begin this journey with a clear focus and a commitment to excellence in the dynamic and demanding world of SEO.

It's going to be more interesting than you think. I promise.

CHAPTER 1

WHAT IS SEO?

Search Engine Optimisation, or SEO, is a *lot* of things. Just look at my table of contents. And yet so many claim to be experts in all things SEO. I hate to ruin the surprise for you, but most of them are *not*.

It's both an art and a science, demanding a blend of creative and analytical skills to elevate a brand's presence in the digital ecosystem. My own extensive journey, weaving through the landscapes of digital marketing, has grounded me in the realities and complexities of SEO. From the corridors of Yahoo! to spearheading digital channel strategy and execution at Friday Agency here in Dublin, my many years in the field have revealed the nuanced layers of SEO.

Defining SEO in Today's Digital Age

At its very essence, SEO is about enhancing a website's visibility in the organic search results of search engines. So, ranking highly on search engines like Google when someone is searching for what you do or sell. Sounds simple, right? This foundational objective might seem straightforward, but it encapsulates a complex interplay of technical acumen and profound understanding of human behaviour online. SEO isn't merely about ensuring your website shows up at the top of search results; it's about grasping what drives people to search in the first place - what they are searching for, the specific words and phrases they use, and the type of content they prefer to engage with. This deep comprehension allows businesses to finely tune their digital content to meet users exactly where they are in their quest for information, solutions, or products.

Understanding the intent behind searches - whether users seek knowledge, specific products, or services - enables organisations to craft content strategies that align precisely with user needs. This alignment is critical not just for attracting traffic but for attracting the right kind of traffic—visitors who are most likely to convert into customers. By delivering relevant and timely content that answers real questions and provides real solutions, businesses can effectively connect with their target audience.

Moreover, SEO transcends the mechanical aspects of marketing. It's about humanising the brand in a digital space, crafting experiences that delight, inform, and engage. Each search query offers a unique opportunity to turn casual interest into meaningful interactions, converting ordinary searchers into engaged users and loyal patrons. This transformation is achieved not through random chance but through a deliberate and thoughtful approach to content that speaks directly to the interests and needs of users.

Beyond drawing visitors, effective SEO helps a business stand out in a saturated market. In today's digital age, where information is abundant and attention spans are short, simply being visible isn't enough. Businesses must distinguish themselves not just for being visible but for being valuable leaders in their space. SEO helps position businesses as thought leaders and trusted providers by ensuring that they are consistently present where and when it matters most.

This aspect of SEO—establishing and reinforcing credibility and trust—cannot be overstated. In a digital marketplace where new competitors can emerge overnight, having a robust online presence that offers consistency, reliability, and authority is invaluable. SEO plays a crucial role in building this presence. It's not just about algorithms and rankings; it's about constructing a digital persona that resonates with authenticity and expertise.

Hence, SEO is as much about people as it is about technical metrics. It's about understanding the subtle nuances of human interaction with technology and leveraging this understanding to not only meet but exceed the expectations of both search engines and searchers. By focusing on people, businesses can turn the mechanical act of searching into a dynamic human interaction—a conversation that fosters engagement and loyalty, and transforms passive viewers into active participants and advocates for the brand. This people-centred approach to SEO makes it an indispensable tool in the digital marketer's toolkit, one that impacts not just web traffic and page rankings but the very relationship between a brand and its customers.

Do You Need SEO?

"We'll go with the new website but we can't afford the SEO right now…"

This statement could have been made ten years ago, but sadly, for some, things haven't changed.

I still hear this. Often. And realistically, if you can't afford to invest in SEO, you can't afford a website. Furthermore, most websites are useless without SEO.

The persistent belief that SEO is an optional add-on rather than a fundamental component of a digital marketing strategy is one of the most damaging misconceptions businesses hold.

Far too often, businesses end up with websites that fail to function as effective sales tools. This typically stems from the erroneous belief that SEO is not essential, that it's an optional extra, or that a modest investment in SEO will suffice. Some even view SEO with scepticism, thinking it's a scam. This perspective is partially fuelled by the behaviour of so-called 'professionals' in the industry who promise the moon but deliver little of value.

SEO drives visibility among those who may not have heard of your brand. Without it, your website mainly attracts traffic from those who already know about you. To put it bluntly, without ongoing investment in SEO, you might as well stand on a street corner and show your new website to passersby on a laptop. That's probably the only way they'll ever see it.

Consider a scenario where you're a new brand, perhaps a startup needing its first website. You gather a few quotes from agencies or developers. Being a startup, you opt for the cheapest option. It seems like a reasonable decision, right? Well, it's not. It's wrong on multiple levels.

Your website needs to be built with SEO in mind from the ground up. Being told that your website will be "SEO-friendly" often means very little. There is no such thing as an inherently "SEO-friendly" website unless a strategic approach to SEO and content is embedded into its development. This strategy should include understanding your business and audience, conducting keyword research, competitor analysis, and performing a content gap analysis. These should all be backed by a robust content strategy and calendar, informed by thorough research.

By research, I don't mean standing with clipboards on Grafton Street in Dublin. This involves conducting surveys of your actual audience, holding focus groups, and utilising a variety of other data collection methods. From this information, you gain insights into what your potential audience wants, particularly in terms of content.

Additionally, it's crucial to find out who your audience is, what makes them tick, where they engage online, and how. All of this information informs your SEO strategy. If you're launching your first website and none of the above has been discussed, then your website is not "SEO-friendly" at all.

Many websites undergo complete overhauls, redesigns, or redevelopments, often changing their URLs and structure. Failing to factor in SEO during these stages will result in lost traffic. There is no question about it.

If you're requesting quotes from digital agencies for a new website and receive one without a recommended investment for SEO, discard it immediately. If you disqualify agencies or developers because SEO is included but seems too expensive, you must reconsider. SEO is essential. Without it, you WILL lose traffic and revenue.

If you're migrating to a new website, SEO is so crucial. When URLs change, even slightly, your previous ones become broken pages. This means any website that previously linked to you, which was likely helping your rankings, now points to a broken page. Your referral traffic that historically generated leads or revenue will also point to broken pages, resulting in lost revenue. You will also lose the benefits of past links to those pages.

Website migration is an ideal time to revise your core SEO elements, such as page titles, descriptions, and rich snippets. However, if SEO is not included in the scope of your project, do not expect this work to be done. Neglecting SEO during a migration can lead to peculiar-looking search results.

Website migration is also the perfect opportunity to introduce new, research-based content. Some of this will come from your overall research initiatives and usability testing. It can also be guided by keyword research specific to the identified audiences. This process ensures that your website not only retains its existing traffic but also stands a better chance of increasing it.

The agency I work for, Friday Agency, recently built a new website for a client, and the increase in SEO users since then has been remarkable. This success was not solely due to SEO. It was a perfect mix of all digital disciplines coming together - research, content, architecture, design, build, and SEO. It was the result of a brand that understands the importance of integrating SEO into every aspect of a new website and migration.

SEO is not optional. It never can be. Without SEO, a new website will rarely be found. Without SEO, a website migration can and likely will - have catastrophic results.

Investing in SEO is not a one-time effort or a static audit that sits on a shelf gathering dust (more on this later). It's a dynamic, ongoing process that requires continual attention, adaptation, and refinement. SEO is your most reliable tool for ensuring sustained visibility, engagement, and growth. Don't let your website become an invisible entity.

Embrace SEO as an integral part of your strategy, and watch your online presence flourish.

The Evolution of SEO: A Personal Recollection

When I embarked on my digital marketing journey, the landscape of SEO was markedly different from what it is today. In those formative years, SEO could be characterised as somewhat simpler, though perhaps less sophisticated and nuanced. The focus was predominantly on keywords, backlinks, and achieving high visibility in search engine results. The strategy was straightforward: populate your content with relevant keywords, accumulate as many backlinks as possible, and watch your page rise to the top of search engine listings.

However, this approach was to evolve dramatically with the passage of time. As the digital landscape expanded and matured, so too did the algorithms that underpinned search engine technologies. The advent of increasingly sophisticated algorithms by major search engines like Google marked a significant shift in the SEO paradigm. No longer was it sufficient to merely stuff a webpage with keywords or amass a large volume of backlinks. The emerging algorithms began to prioritise the intent behind search queries, the quality and relevance of the content, and the overall user experience. This evolution signalled a move towards a more holistic, nuanced approach to SEO, where the quality of engagement with content became as important, if not more so, than the quantity of keywords or links.

Throughout my career, particularly as I transitioned to roles predominantly on the agency side, I gained a deeper, more comprehensive understanding of the multi-faceted nature of digital marketing. My work across various sectors allowed me to explore how SEO interacts with and is influenced by other elements of the digital marketing spectrum, such as content strategy, social media marketing, User Experience, and even emerging fields like cyberpsychology.

This broad exposure was instrumental in shaping my appreciation of SEO not as a standalone tool but as a component of a larger, integrated digital toolkit. I learned that effective SEO strategies must go beyond mere technical optimisation to include strategic content creation, audience engagement, and a deep understanding of consumer behaviour and expectations. This integrated approach emphasised the importance of creating content that resonates on a human level, content that is crafted not just to rank well but to genuinely engage and convert.

As I continued to delve into the intricacies of SEO, it became clear that understanding and adapting to the changing algorithms was crucial. Each major update by search engines offered new challenges and opportunities to refine and adapt SEO strategies. For instance, Google's Panda and Penguin updates redefined what constituted high-quality content and ethical link-building practices, respectively. Such updates necessitated a shift towards more ethical, sustainable SEO practices that prioritise long-term success over short-term gains.

The integration of SEO with broader digital marketing strategies also highlighted the importance of a cohesive approach that leverages the strengths of each channel. Whether through the strategic use of social media to boost SEO efforts or the application of SEO principles to enhance email marketing campaigns, the interconnectedness of digital channels demanded a more sophisticated, holistic approach to digital marketing.

In retrospect, the evolution of SEO from a purely technical endeavour to a complex, nuanced discipline reflects the broader transformations within the digital marketing industry. It underscores the need for marketers to remain agile, informed, and responsive to the continuous changes in technology and consumer behaviour. As we look towards the future, the lessons learned from the past will undoubtedly continue to influence how we understand and practice SEO, ensuring that it remains a vital, effective tool in the digital marketer's arsenal.

Debunking SEO Myths

In writing this book, one of my primary goals is to dispel the numerous myths that have proliferated around SEO. So you'll see plenty of that. The digital marketing realm is saturated with misconceptions— misguided beliefs that often promise immediate gains, miraculous ranking boosts, and other dubious SEO shortcuts. These myths can not only mislead but can also damage the credibility and long-term success of your online presence. However, understanding the true nature of SEO involves recognising that it is indeed a marathon and not a sprint. Effective SEO requires a blend of patience, persistence, and a profound understanding of the continuously evolving algorithms that power search engines.

For instance, one pervasive myth that I have encountered repeatedly in my two decades in digital marketing is the notion that SEO is about manipulating or tricking search engines. This myth suggests that through certain tricks or hacks, one can fool search engines into giving a website a higher ranking. However, this is far from the truth. Effective SEO is not about deception or manipulation. Instead, it's about forming a partnership with search engines to serve the best possible content to users. This involves adhering to established best practices, focusing intently on the quality of content, and consistently delivering real value to the end-user.

This myth about tricking search engines likely stems from the early days of SEO when many so-called "black hat" techniques—such as keyword stuffing, cloaking, and using invisible text—were employed to gain an undue advantage in search rankings. Over time, however, search engines, particularly Google, have become incredibly sophisticated. They have developed algorithms designed to penalise these manipulative tactics and reward websites that offer genuine value to users through high-quality content and legitimate SEO practices.

In addition to the myth about tricking search engines, there are several other misconceptions I aim to clarify through this book. For example, another common myth is that SEO is solely about keywords. While keywords are undoubtedly important, modern SEO transcends mere keyword optimisation. Today, SEO encompasses a wider array of components including site architecture, authoritative content, mobile compatibility, user experience (UX), and even the security of your site. These elements are crucial for a holistic SEO strategy that appeals to both search engines and users.

Moreover, another myth is the overemphasis on the technical aspects of SEO at the expense of content quality. While technical SEO is important, the heart of SEO is creating compelling, useful, and informative content. Search engines are increasingly capable of assessing the intent behind users' queries and the contextual relevance of content. Therefore, delivering content that accurately and effectively addresses users' needs is paramount.

Furthermore, there is the misconception that SEO results are instant. Many come to SEO with the expectation of quick results—improved rankings, increased traffic, and higher conversions overnight. However, SEO is inherently a long-term strategy. Significant improvements in search visibility require time, during which consistent effort must be applied to optimise various elements of your website and content. The fruits of SEO labour are most often seen over months and years, not days or weeks.

By tackling the correct methods, and therefore these myths, head-on, this book aims to provide a clear, accurate understanding of what SEO involves. It is designed to equip you with the knowledge and strategies necessary for a genuine and sustainable competitive edge in search engines. This is not just about optimising for search engines but optimising for people—creating meaningful experiences that resonate with users and foster long-term loyalty and engagement.

Best Practices and Advanced Techniques

Staying ahead in the dynamic and ever-evolving field of SEO requires a commitment to ongoing education and adaptability. As the digital landscape shifts, driven by technological advances and changes in user behaviour, marketers must be vigilant, continuously updating their strategies to align with the latest trends and search engine algorithm updates. This process involves an ongoing cycle of learning, testing, and adapting to new information and tools that can enhance SEO effectiveness.

The importance of staying updated cannot be overstated. For instance, the rapid adoption of mobile devices over the past decade has revolutionised the approach to website design. Mobile optimisation, once considered an additional feature, has now become a cornerstone of SEO strategy. This shift was largely catalysed by changes in user behaviour, with a significant increase in mobile search queries prompting search engines to adapt their algorithms to prioritise mobile-friendly websites. As a result, SEO strategies had to evolve to ensure websites were optimised for mobile to maintain or improve their search engine rankings.

Voice search is another transformative trend that has reshaped how we think about SEO, particularly in the context of keywords and content structure. As voice-activated devices become more prevalent, the nature of search queries has evolved to become more conversational. This change challenges the traditional keyword-based strategies and calls for a more nuanced approach to content that can interpret and respond to the natural language queries used in voice search. The integration of voice search into SEO strategies exemplifies the need for SEO practitioners to stay current with technological advancements and adjust their tactics accordingly.

Moreover, the application of Artificial Intelligence (AI) in SEO represents a significant frontier for exploration and growth. AI technologies offer profound capabilities in areas such as keyword research, user behaviour prediction, and personalised content creation. These tools can analyse vast amounts of data at incredible speeds, providing insights that would be impossible for humans to generate on their own. As someone with a keen interest in the intersection of AI and marketing, I see immense potential in harnessing AI to refine and enhance SEO strategies. AI-driven analytics can uncover patterns and insights that inform smarter, more effective SEO tactics tailored to the specific preferences and behaviours of target audiences.

However, while AI can dramatically enhance the efficiency and effectiveness of SEO strategies, it is essential to remember that it serves as a complement to, not a replacement for, human expertise. The strategic oversight, creative input, and ethical considerations necessary in SEO require a human touch. AI tools provide support and augment capabilities, but the core of SEO strategy design and decision-making must remain a fundamentally human endeavour.

This continual adaptation to new technologies and shifts in user behaviour underscores the broader narrative of SEO as a discipline that is both reactive and proactive. SEO experts must not only respond to changes as they occur but also anticipate future trends and prepare to integrate new practices that align with where technology and user behaviour are headed. This proactive approach ensures that SEO strategies remain effective and competitive, even as the digital landscape continues to evolve.

In sum, staying ahead in SEO isn't just about keeping pace with current trends—it's about foreseeing the future of technology and search behaviour, and adapting strategies proactively to maintain a competitive edge. This requires a blend of continuous learning, practical application, and forward-thinking that is essential for anyone looking to excel in the complex and challenging world of search engine optimisation.

SEO as a Reflection of Consumer Behaviour

Understanding the deep connection between SEO and consumer behaviour unlocks a fascinating realm where technology meets human psychology. This chapter explores how SEO not only adapts to but also reflects the intricacies of how consumers interact with digital content, make decisions, and ultimately engage with brands online.

The Psychological Underpinnings of Search

At its core, every search query is driven by a human desire or need. Whether a person is looking for the nearest coffee shop, how to fix a leaky tap, or the best digital marketing strategies, each search reflects an underlying aspect of consumer behaviour. By analysing these behaviours, SEO professionals can craft strategies that not only address the user's immediate needs but also anticipate future inquiries and interactions.

The process begins with understanding the 'search intent'—the purpose behind every search query. Search intent can be broadly categorised into informational, navigational, transactional, and commercial investigations. Each category reflects a different mindset of the searcher:

Informational Searches: Looking for information without any immediate intent to purchase. Users might be gathering information to help them solve a problem or satisfy curiosity.

Navigational Searches: Trying to locate a specific website or page. This reflects brand recognition and familiarity.

Transactional Searches: Ready to buy or perform another specific web action. This shows a direct intent to engage with products or services.

Commercial Investigation: Considering a purchase and looking for the best options or reviews. This indicates decision-making processes in play.

By mapping content and SEO strategies to these different intents, marketers can more effectively align their offerings with the user's specific stage in the buying journey.

Understanding the psychological triggers that influence online behaviour can greatly enhance how content is crafted and presented. Factors such as urgency, authority, and emotion play significant roles in how content is received and acted upon. For example, content that creates a sense of urgency (e.g., limited-time offers) can drive quicker decision-making in transactional searches. Similarly, content that establishes authority and trustworthiness—such as detailed guides, citations from reputable sources, and expert opinions—can be more persuasive in informational and commercial investigation scenarios.

Moreover, the emotional appeal of content can significantly impact user engagement. Content that resonates on an emotional level can increase the likelihood of shares and interactions, especially on social media platforms. SEO strategies that incorporate emotional elements, such as stories or relatable experiences, can thus perform better in terms of both engagement and conversion.

In an era dominated by concerns over data privacy, personalised marketing must tread a fine line between customisation and intrusion. The introduction of stringent data protection regulations like GDPR has made the task of personalising content without overstepping legal boundaries more challenging yet more critical than ever.

SEO, when done correctly, respects these boundaries while still offering tailored experiences. This is achieved through strategies like user segmentation that does not rely on personally identifiable information, and context-based targeting which looks at situational factors rather than personal data. For instance, adjusting content based on the time of day, current weather conditions, or widely observed events can provide personalisation in a privacy-conscious manner.

The intersection of SEO and consumer behaviour is poised to become even more complex and intertwined. Advances in AI and machine learning are making it possible to predict user behaviour with greater accuracy. For example, AI can analyse vast amounts of data from search trends to identify emerging patterns that may not be immediately obvious. This capability allows for proactive content strategies that anticipate user needs and optimise content dynamically.

SEO as a reflection of consumer behaviour offers a rich landscape for exploration and innovation. By understanding the psychological factors that drive search behaviours, SEO professionals can create more effective and engaging online experiences. This chapter not only delves into these dynamics but also provides actionable insights that leverage these behaviours to improve both search visibility and user satisfaction. As we continue to navigate the evolving digital landscape, the link between consumer behaviour and SEO will undoubtedly play a pivotal role in shaping the future of digital marketing.

Looking Forward

As we look to the future, the intricate role of SEO within the broad tapestry of digital marketing continues to expand and evolve, becoming increasingly vital to successful marketing strategies. The rapid advancements in Artificial Intelligence (AI), the growing prominence of voice and visual search technologies, and the perpetual evolution of search engine algorithms are reshaping the landscape, compelling SEO professionals to adopt more sophisticated, integrated approaches.

The SEO landscape today bears little resemblance to its earlier form when I began my digital marketing journey. Back then, it was a nascent field dominated by relatively straightforward tactics focused on keywords and backlinks. Now, it has matured into a dynamic domain that requires a harmonious blend of technical expertise, creative insight, and an in-depth understanding of consumer psychology. This evolution reflects broader shifts in technology and user expectations, driving SEO professionals to not only react to changes but also anticipate and prepare for future developments.

In this evolving digital environment, the ability to adapt and foresee trends is crucial. For instance, the integration of AI into SEO practices is not just about automating tasks but about enhancing the understanding of user intent and improving the personalisation of content. AI's ability to analyse data at scale offers unprecedented insights that can refine SEO strategies, making them more effective and user-centric.

Moreover, the rise of voice search and the increasing importance of visual content demand a re-evaluation of traditional SEO strategies. Voice search optimisation requires a deep understanding of natural language processing to cater to the more conversational tone of voice queries, while visual search necessitates optimising images and videos to be more discoverable and engaging. These shifts underscore the need for SEO strategies that are flexible and adaptable to new technologies and changing user behaviours.

Additionally, as the regulatory landscape around data privacy continues to tighten with frameworks like GDPR, SEO strategies must also evolve to ensure compliance while still delivering personalised user experiences. This necessitates a delicate balance between leveraging user data for personalisation and respecting user privacy, a challenge that requires both creative solutions and a thorough understanding of privacy regulations.

This book is designed to equip you with the knowledge and tools necessary to navigate these complex waters. By merging foundational SEO principles with advanced techniques and emerging trends, I aim to provide a comprehensive guide that prepares you for both the present challenges and future opportunities in SEO. This approach will not only enhance your immediate SEO efforts but also ensure that your strategies are sustainable and effective in the long term, helping you to not just compete, but excel in the increasingly complex world of digital marketing.

If you're still paying attention, that is.

CHAPTER 2

HOW SEARCH ENGINES WORK

Let's get back to basics. Understanding the inner workings of search engine algorithms is crucial for any SEO professional. These algorithms are the heartbeat of search engines, dictating the dynamics of digital visibility. They are complex systems designed to retrieve data from the search index and instantly deliver the best possible results for a query. This section provides a deep dive into the world of search engine algorithms, exploring their evolution, how they operate today, and their impact on SEO strategies.

Evolution of Search Engine Algorithms

The history of search engine algorithms is as old as search engines themselves. Obviously. In the early days of the internet, search engines like AltaVista and Yahoo! used relatively simple algorithms based on keyword density to rank websites. However, these systems were easy to manipulate, leading to a poor user experience filled with spammy content.

Google revolutionised this landscape in the late 1990s with the introduction of the PageRank algorithm, which assessed the quality and quantity of backlinks to determine a webpage's importance. This was a fundamental shift from previous methods because it introduced the concept of webpage authority, drastically reducing the effectiveness of keyword stuffing and promoting a more organic growth of internet content quality.

Over the years, Google and other search engines have continuously refined their algorithms to better understand and satisfy user intent. Updates like Google's Panda, Penguin, and Hummingbird, and more recent ones like BERT and RankBrain, have been developed to improve the relevance and quality of search results. These updates focus on various aspects, from penalising poor quality content and spammy link practices to utilising natural language processing to understand the context of queries better.

How Search Engine Algorithms Work Today

Modern search engine algorithms are highly sophisticated and take into account hundreds, if not thousands, of different factors when ranking web pages. These algorithms are designed to perform several tasks:

Crawling: This is the process by which search engines use bots (also known as spiders) to collect information about all the content available on the internet. The crawler starts from a known web page and follows internal links to other pages on the same site, as well as external links to different websites.

Indexing: After a page is crawled, the data is parsed and stored in a vast database, or index. This index is essentially a giant library of all the crawled web content and their associated keywords.

Processing Queries: When a user enters a search query, the search engine algorithms retrieve relevant content from this index. The relevancy is determined based on several factors, including keywords, site usability, and user engagement metrics.

Ranking: The final step is the ranking of retrieved web pages in order of relevance. This is where the algorithm's assessment of hundreds of ranking factors comes into play, including page speed, mobile-friendliness, content quality, user experience, and much more.

Impact on SEO Strategies

Understanding how search engine algorithms function is essential for developing effective SEO strategies. Since these algorithms are geared toward enhancing the user experience by providing the most relevant and high-quality content, SEO efforts must align with these goals.

For instance, the emphasis on quality content and user engagement metrics means that SEO strategies must go beyond mere keyword optimisation to include producing valuable content that genuinely addresses the needs and questions of users. Additionally, as mobile usage continues to grow, mobile optimisation has become a crucial ranking factor, influencing SEO practices to ensure websites are responsive and mobile-friendly.

Moreover, the use of AI and machine learning by search engines to refine their algorithms means that SEO strategies must also evolve to be more data-driven. AI tools can help in understanding pattern changes in user behaviour and predicting shifts in SEO trends, allowing marketers to adapt more dynamically to the changing landscape.

The complexity of search engine algorithms requires that SEO professionals maintain a thorough understanding of both the technical and content-driven aspects of SEO. This knowledge is not only crucial for adapting to the current digital environment but also for anticipating future changes, ensuring that SEO strategies remain effective and aligned with the core objective of search engines: to deliver the best user experience by surfacing the most relevant and authoritative content.

Crawling, Indexing, and Ranking Processes

Let's dive into the nitty-gritty of how search engines work—specifically, how they crawl, index, and rank content. These processes are the backbone of any effective SEO strategy, and understanding them can be your ace in the hole for outmanoeuvring competitors and capturing that coveted top spot in search results.

Crawling: The Discovery Phase

First up in the SEO process, we have crawling. Imagine a search engine as a tireless explorer navigating the vast expanse of the digital world. This explorer, more technically known as a web crawler and affectionately dubbed a spider, embarks on a critical mission to scour the Internet to discover and revisit web pages. The journey begins with a predefined map— a list of web addresses gleaned from previous crawls along with sitemaps submitted by websites. This list acts much like a seasoned hiker's favourite trails, familiar yet full of potential for new discoveries.

As this digital explorer ventures through the web, it meticulously inspects new and updated content. It examines each webpage it encounters, making note of any changes or new information since its last visit. This includes scrutinising the links contained within the pages, which the crawler uses like breadcrumbs leading to new destinations. Each link uncovers a path to potentially undiscovered content, expanding the crawler's map and enriching the search engine's expansive index.

This crawling process is absolutely fundamental. Without it, a webpage is invisible to the search engine and, by extension, to the vast majority of potential visitors. It's akin to a tree falling in a deserted forest; without a witness, does it make a sound? Similarly, if a page isn't crawled, does it even exist online? The answer, for all intents and purposes, is no — not in the world where visibility through search engines drives traffic and engagement.

Ensuring your website is crawler-friendly, therefore, is not just important—it's a critical necessity in SEO. This means your website's structure must be navigable and clear, not just to human visitors but to web crawlers that depend on easily accessible links to perform their duties effectively. Each page should be well-connected through logical, straightforward links that guide the crawler from one page to another and back again. Think of your website as a city laid out for a marathon; you want to provide clear, unobstructed paths that lead runners (crawlers) smoothly from start to finish without any confusion.

Moreover, the importance of a robust sitemap cannot be overstated. A sitemap acts like a guidebook for crawlers; it presents a complete list of the pages on your site, ensuring that crawlers know about all the pages, including those that might be newly added or only infrequently linked to from other areas of your site. By submitting this to search engines, you essentially hand them a map, highlighting all the stops along the way, ensuring none of your content is overlooked.

Accessibility is another crucial aspect. This not only means that links should be working and direct to the correct pages, but also that your site's architecture supports crawler efficiency. Using proper HTML markup, ensuring that AJAX and JavaScript elements on your site are crawlable, and avoiding the creation of cul-de-sacs where crawlers get stuck and can't exit from a page are all strategic necessities.

To sum up, the crawling phase of SEO is like laying down the foundational stones of a building. Just as a building needs a solid foundation to stand, your website needs thorough and efficient crawling to be seen. It's about making sure that the paths are clear, the map is comprehensive, and the terrain is accessible. With these elements in place, you set the stage for successful indexing and ranking, which ultimately determines how visible and effective your online presence will be.

Indexing: The Organising Phase

Moving from the dynamic activity of crawling, we enter the methodical world of indexing. Once a web crawler has discovered a page, the content must be processed and organised. This is where indexing comes into play. You can think of indexing much like cataloguing books in an extensive, infinitely detailed library. Each webpage, much like a book in this analogy, must find its appropriate place on the library's shelves.

How Indexing Works

The indexing process begins once the crawler submits the data it has collected. Each element of the webpage is meticulously analysed and stored in a vast database, known as an index. This index is not just a simple list; it's an elaborate, highly organised structure that allows search engines to retrieve information swiftly and efficiently.

During indexing, a search engine processes the content of each page to understand and store its contents comprehensively. It dissects the text, images, videos, and any other multimedia elements, extracting information about the page's structure, the relevance of content, the context of information, and the relationships between various elements.

Cataloguing Content

The search engine's algorithms analyse various components of the page, such as:

Page Titles and Headings: These are often the first elements looked at, as they provide a concise summary of the content.

Meta Descriptions: These brief page descriptions are crucial as they offer a snapshot of what the page is about, often used directly in search engine results.

Keywords: While not as dominant a factor as in the early days of SEO, keywords still play a significant role in helping determine the topic and relevance of the content.

Alt Text for Images: This text helps search engines understand what images are about since they can't "see" images the way a human would.

Structured Data: This markup helps search engines understand the context of the information provided on the page, such as articles, reviews, and product information.

Each piece of data is catalogued and indexed according to its content and relevance. This meticulous organisation ensures that when a search query is processed, the search engine can quickly sift through billions of pages in the index to find the most relevant results.

Optimising for Indexing

For SEO professionals and webmasters, understanding the indexing process is critical because it underscores the importance of optimising web pages. To ensure that your pages are not just indexed but also well-positioned within the index, consider the following strategies:

Clear, Descriptive Titles and Headings: Make sure these are reflective of the content and structured in a way that highlights the main topics and subtopics.

Accurate Meta Descriptions: Craft meta descriptions that effectively summarise the page content and entice users to click through from the search results.

Relevant Keywords: Include pertinent keywords naturally within the content, especially in titles, headings, and near the top of the content to reinforce the themes of your pages.

Rich Media Descriptions: Always use alt text for images and provide transcripts for video and audio content, as this helps index and understand multimedia content which cannot be 'read' directly by search engines.

Implement Structured Data: Use schema markup to help search engines interpret and display your content in an enhanced manner, such as in featured snippets or rich results.

By ensuring your content is well-optimised and clearly structured, you make it easier for search engines to not only index your pages accurately but also understand their context and relevance. This detailed organisation within the index is what allows your content to be surfaced when users make queries that your pages can answer effectively.

The Impact of a Well-Organised Index

A well-organised index is crucial for the efficacy of search results. It ensures that users are provided with the most relevant and high-quality content for their searches. For content creators and SEO professionals, a deep understanding of the indexing process and its requirements is not just beneficial—it's essential for ensuring that their content finds its rightful place in the vast library that is the internet, readily accessible and correctly positioned to meet the needs of users. This is the cornerstone of effective SEO and is what makes a site not just visible, but valuable in the eyes of both search engines and searchers.

Ranking: The Judging Phase

Finally, we arrive at the ranking process, arguably the most crucial and dynamic phase of SEO. This is where the magic of search engines truly manifests. Once the content is crawled and indexed, it enters the competitive arena of ranking, where it must prove its worth against countless other pages. The search engines act as the ultimate judges in this digital talent show, determining which pages are most relevant to a user's query and should thus be featured prominently in the search results.

Understanding Ranking Signals

The decision to rank web pages is based on a complex interplay of hundreds of ranking signals. These signals are the criteria search engines use to evaluate and compare web pages. They can range from the technical aspects of a website to the quality and engagement metrics of its content. Key ranking signals include:

Content Relevance: How well the content of the page matches the user's search query. This involves the use of targeted keywords, the depth of topic coverage, and the freshness of the content.

Page Loading Speed: How quickly a page loads on both desktop and mobile devices. Faster loading times improve user experience and are favoured by search engines.

Mobile-Friendliness: How well a webpage is optimised for mobile devices. As mobile searches continue to rise, this factor has become increasingly critical in ranking algorithms.

User Engagement: Metrics such as time spent on page, engagement rates, and interaction rates that indicate how users are engaging with the content. High engagement rates are often indicative of content quality and relevance.

Backlinks: The number and quality of backlinks pointing to a page. Links from reputable and relevant sources can significantly enhance a page's authority and ranking.

User Experience (UX): Factors including site architecture, navigation, and visual appeal, which affect how users interact with a page. A positive user experience is essential for retaining visitors and converting them into repeat users.

As an SEO strategist, envision yourself as a coach preparing your contestants for the big show. Your web pages are your team, and each member needs to be finely tuned and well-prepared to meet the judges' rigorous standards. Here's how you can ensure your pages are competition-ready:

Optimise for Relevance: Tailor your content to meet the specific needs and questions of your target audience. Use keyword research to align your content closely with the common and trending queries related to your topic.

Enhance Performance: Work on the technical aspects of your site to improve page loading speeds. Optimise images, leverage browser caching, and minimise the use of blocking resources.

Prioritise Mobile Optimisation: Ensure that your website offers a seamless experience on mobile devices. Responsive design and mobile-friendly layouts are non-negotiable in today's mobile-first world.

Engage Your Audience: Create compelling content that captivates and engages. Utilise formats that encourage interaction, such as videos, infographics, and interactive polls.

Build Authority with Backlinks: Cultivate high-quality backlinks from authoritative sources. Guest blogging, collaborations, and creating shareable content are effective strategies for building a robust backlink profile.

Refine User Experience: Continuously test and improve the user experience of your site. Simple navigation, a clean layout, and engaging visuals all contribute to a positive user experience that can keep visitors coming back.

The Ever-Evolving Nature of SEO

Remember, SEO is not a static field; what works today may not work tomorrow. Search engines are continually refining their algorithms to better serve user needs, which means the criteria and weight of ranking signals can change. Keeping abreast of these changes and adapting your strategies accordingly is essential for maintaining and improving your search engine rankings.

The ranking process is where your SEO efforts culminate, and it's where you see the results of your hard work in the visibility and performance of your web pages. By understanding the intricacies of ranking signals and diligently optimising your content and website, you can ensure that your pages not only show up but truly stand out in the crowded space of search engine results. This is your opportunity to shine in the spotlight of the digital stage and make a lasting impression on your audience.

Understanding and optimising for the fundamental SEO processes of crawling, indexing, and ranking is not just about enhancing visibility; it's about distinguishing your digital presence in a sea of mediocrity. Mastering these elements can propel your website from the shadows of obscurity to the bright lights of the first page of search results. And let's be frank—being a superstar in the search results isn't just good for your ego; it's critical for your business's success in the digital era.

In the grand theatre of digital marketing, SEO is your spotlight. Without it, no matter how good your act might be, you're just another unnoticed performer on a dark stage. By mastering the intricacies of crawling, indexing, and ranking, you're not just aiming for a brief appearance in the search results; you're gearing up for a sustained run at the top.

And let's be honest, we're here to grab that spotlight and shine. So let's roll up our sleeves and prepare your pages for their standing ovation. It's about making sure that when your audience searches for relevant topics, yours isn't just another face in the digital crowd, but the star of the show, commanding attention and drawing crowds. Optimising these fundamental SEO processes ensures your content not only reaches your audience but also resonates and engages them at a higher level, turning casual visitors into loyal fans.

In summary, understanding and optimising for crawling, indexing, and ranking are pivotal to securing a successful digital presence. By refining these processes, you set the stage for enhanced visibility, better user engagement, and ultimately, superior conversion rates. So let's get your pages ready for their standing ovation and ensure your site not only participates in the digital marketplace but truly stands out and thrives.

CHAPTER 3
UNDERSTANDING YOUR AUDIENCE

In the vast landscape of digital marketing, understanding who your audience is plays a pivotal role in the success of your SEO strategies and overall marketing efforts. Identifying target demographics involves more than just knowing who your customers are; it's about understanding their behaviours, preferences, and needs at a granular level. This section of the book delves deep into the processes and strategies for identifying your target demographics, ensuring that every marketing move you make is informed and effective.

The Importance of Knowing Your Audience

Before diving into the mechanics of identifying your audience, it's crucial to acknowledge why this knowledge is foundational. Understanding your target demographics helps tailor your content, design, and marketing strategies to meet the specific needs and preferences of your audience. This customisation not only enhances user engagement but also significantly boosts the effectiveness of your SEO efforts by attracting more qualified traffic, improving conversion rates, and ultimately, increasing ROI.

Start with Broad Segments

Identifying your target demographics often starts with broad categorisations such as age, gender, location, and income level. These basic demographic factors can provide a good starting point for understanding who your audience is. For example, a brand selling luxury goods might target higher income levels, while a university might focus on younger age groups in specific geographic regions.

Age and Gender: Knowing the age range and gender of your audience can help in creating content that resonates with them. For instance, younger audiences might prefer more visually engaging content and a casual tone, while older demographics might appreciate more detailed, information-rich content.

Location: Geographical targeting is essential, especially for local SEO. Understanding where your audience lives can help tailor your SEO to focus on location-specific keywords and customise your content to reflect local interests and cultural nuances.

Income Level: This helps in pitching your products or services in a way that aligns with the economic capabilities of your audience. Luxury brands, budget services, and mid-tier products all speak to different income groups.

Dive into Psychographics

While demographics give you a broad outline of who your audience might be, psychographics allow you to delve deeper into the why. Psychographics pertain to the psychological attributes of your audience, including their personalities, values, opinions, attitudes, interests, and lifestyles.

Personality Traits: Are your customers risk-takers or more conservative? Understanding personality can help you craft messages that resonate emotionally and intellectually.

Values and Beliefs: These are especially important in today's socially conscious market. For instance, a brand that sells eco-friendly products would benefit from targeting consumers who value sustainability.

Interests and Hobbies: These details can help you create content that appeals to what your audience enjoys. For example, if you're marketing a sports brand, content that ties into major sporting events or fitness trends would likely be compelling.

Utilising Data and Tools

To accurately identify your target demographics, leverage both quantitative and qualitative data. Here are some tools and methodologies to aid in this process:

Analytics Tools: Use tools like Google Analytics, which provide insights into who is visiting your website, what content they are interacting with, and their pathways through your site.

Social Media Insights: Platforms like Facebook, Instagram, and Twitter offer in-depth analytics that can help you understand the demographics and interests of your followers and those interacting with your content.

Surveys and Feedback: Directly asking your audience through surveys or feedback forms can provide explicit information about their preferences and needs.

Market Research: Comprehensive market research, including competitor analysis and industry trends, can offer broader insights into target demographics.

Segmentation Tools: Tools that segment your audience based on their online behaviour, purchasing history, and engagement with past content can provide a dynamic view of your audience's preferences.

Applying Demographic Insights to SEO

Once you have thoroughly delineated and understood your target demographics, the real work begins—integrating this knowledge into your SEO and broader digital marketing strategies. This involves an intricate process of fine-tuning your approach to ensure it resonates with the specific traits, behaviours, and preferences of your audience. Each step, from keyword research to content customisation and channel optimisation, must be deliberately shaped to meet the nuanced needs of your demographic segments.

Tailoring Your SEO Strategy

Keyword research is the cornerstone of effective SEO, serving as the foundation upon which your content strategy is built. When you have a clear grasp of your target demographics, you can refine your keyword research to align with the language and search behaviours specific to your audience. This means moving beyond generic, high-competition keywords to more nuanced phrases that your specific audience might use. For instance, younger demographics might use more colloquial phrases or trending terms, while professional or older segments may use more formal language.

Utilise tools like Google's Keyword Planner, Ahrefs, or SEMrush to analyse keyword trends and search volumes based on demographic data. Consider incorporating regional slang or local terminology if you're targeting specific geographic areas. The goal here is to think like your audience, using the words and phrases they use, to enhance the visibility of your content in search results that matter to them.

Customising Content

With an understanding of your audience's pain points, desires, and information needs, customise your content to speak directly to these elements. This isn't just about what you say, but how you say it. Content should be crafted in a tone and style that connects with your demographic. For example, if targeting tech-savvy millennials, a casual and informative tone with up-to-date information and digital trends will likely resonate well. In contrast, a more professional and detailed approach might be better suited for business executives or industry professionals.

Your content should also address the specific questions and concerns of your audience. Use the insights from your demographic research to guide the topics you cover, ensuring they are relevant and engaging. Create content formats that appeal to your audience—whether that's detailed blog posts, engaging videos, infographics, or interactive content. The more your content aligns with the interests and preferences of your audience, the more likely it is to engage and convert.

Optimising Marketing Channels

Knowing where your audience spends their time online guides where you should focus your marketing efforts. Different demographics cluster on different platforms and respond to different types of media. For instance, if your target audience primarily consists of professionals, LinkedIn and industry-specific forums might be the most effective channels. Conversely, if you're targeting a younger, more visually-oriented audience, platforms like Instagram and TikTok might yield better engagement.

Channel optimisation also involves ensuring that your messages are appropriately formatted for each platform, taking into account the unique characteristics of each. For example, what works on Twitter will not necessarily work on Facebook. Each platform has its best practices for content, such as optimal posting times, content length, and multimedia usage, which should be adhered to maximise engagement.

The Impact of Deep Demographic Understanding

Grasping the subtleties of your target demographics transforms how you approach digital marketing and SEO. It allows for a more tailored, strategic approach that not only captures attention but also drives engagement and conversions. This deep demographic insight acts as a compass guiding your content creation, keyword strategy, and channel optimisation, ensuring that every marketing move you make is calculated and impactful.

By thoroughly aligning your SEO and marketing strategies with the characteristics and preferences of your audience, you elevate your digital presence to new heights. It's not just about being seen; it's about being recognised as a trusted, relevant source that meets the specific needs of your audience. This alignment not only increases the effectiveness of your digital marketing efforts but also enhances user satisfaction and loyalty, which are critical components of long-term success in the digital realm.

In essence, understanding and identifying your target demographics is a continuous, dynamic process that refines and perfects your marketing strategy. It is an essential practice for any marketer aiming to not just compete but lead in the highly competitive digital marketplace. By focusing on the nuanced needs and behaviours of your audience, you can ensure that your brand not only attracts but profoundly engages and resonates with the people you aim to serve.

Understanding User Intent and Behaviour

Delving deeper into the essence of effective SEO and digital marketing, we come to the critical concepts of user intent and behaviour. Grasping these concepts is essential for tailoring your digital strategies to meet the actual needs and expectations of your audience. This section explores the nuances of user intent, the various types of behaviours exhibited by users while searching online, and the tools you can use to gather meaningful insights into these dynamics.

The Spectrum of User Intent

User intent refers to the purpose behind a user's search query. Understanding this intent is crucial because it dictates the kind of content you should create to satisfy user needs and how you can optimise it to enhance visibility and engagement. Typically, user intent can be categorised into four main types:

Informational Intent: Users with informational intent are primarily looking for information. Their queries might include words like "how to," "what is," or "guide on" — for example, "how to tie a tie" or "what is blockchain technology?" Content that answers these questions directly and comprehensively performs well for these queries.

Navigational Intent: This intent involves users searching for a specific website or page. Here, the user already knows where they want to go; they just use the search engine as a shortcut. Examples include "Facebook login" or "Amazon homepage." For these queries, ensuring your brand is optimally positioned is key.

Transactional Intent: Users with transactional intent are ready to buy or engage in another type of transaction. Their searches are likely to include terms like "buy," "deal," "discount," or specific product names. For these users, your content needs to be sales-oriented, with clear calls-to-action and streamlined purchasing processes.

Commercial Investigation: Users in this category are considering a purchase and are looking more deeply into their options. They may search for comparisons or reviews, like "best DSLR cameras 2024" or "iPhone vs. Android reviews." Content that helps these users make informed decisions, such as comparative analyses and detailed reviews, will be most effective.

Analysing User Behaviour

Beyond understanding user intent, analysing how users behave when they interact with your content is equally important. This involves looking at metrics such as:

Click-Through Rates (CTR): How often users click on your content after seeing it in search results. Low CTRs may indicate that your titles or meta descriptions are not compelling enough or not well aligned with search intent.

Bounce Rates: The percentage of visitors who leave your site after viewing only one page. A high bounce rate might suggest that your content is not satisfying user needs, or your page is not user-friendly.

Conversion Rates: The percentage of users who take a desired action on your site, such as making a purchase or signing up for a newsletter. This metric helps gauge the effectiveness of your content in driving desired outcomes.

Tools for Audience Research

Several tools are available to help you understand user intent and behaviour more deeply, providing insights that can sharpen your SEO and content strategies:

Google Analytics: Offers comprehensive insights into how users find and interact with your site, including detailed behaviour flow charts, conversion metrics, and audience demographics.

Google Search Console: Provides data on how your site performs in search results, including the queries that bring users to your site, your content's average ranking, and your CTR for specific queries.

SEMrush: A versatile tool that offers features for keyword research, competitive analysis, and more. It helps you understand what users are searching for and how they interact with similar content across the web.

Ahrefs: Great for examining your site's link profile and conducting keyword research. It also offers a content explorer tool that helps you see what content in your niche performs best for particular queries.

BuzzSumo: Useful for analysing which types of content get the most engagement and shares. It helps gauge the types of headlines, topics, and content formats that resonate most with your audience.

By effectively utilising these powerful tools, I can gain a clearer and more detailed picture of my audience's needs and expectations. This insight is invaluable, as it allows me to create content that resonates deeply with my audience, capturing their interest right from the start and holding it through to the final call to action. But my job doesn't stop at just attracting users; it's about creating a user experience that keeps them coming back for more. This means producing content that not only answers their immediate questions but also engages them on a deeper level, encouraging interaction, discussion, and sharing.

Understanding user intent and behaviour is not merely a checkbox in the complex SEO process. It's an ongoing dialogue with your audience. As I continue to listen and respond to their needs, I find that my content becomes more refined and targeted, which in turn fosters deeper engagement and drives higher conversion rates. For instance, if I notice through analytics that a particular type of content performs well in terms of user engagement and conversion, I will focus more energy on developing similar content, refining the approach based on user feedback and interaction data.

Furthermore, the digital landscape is ever-evolving, with new technologies, platforms, and user preferences emerging regularly. Therefore, understanding user intent and behaviour isn't a static task—it requires continuous observation and adaptation. I keep my strategies agile, ready to pivot or adjust based on new data and evolving trends. This might mean adopting new SEO tools that offer more advanced insights, experimenting with different content formats to see what resonates, or even revising my website's navigation to improve user experience based on how users interact with my content.

This ongoing effort is absolutely key to maintaining a robust and effective digital presence that stays closely aligned with the needs of my target audience. By committing to this continuous process of learning and adaptation, I ensure that my digital strategies remain effective and relevant. This approach not only helps in achieving high rankings in search results but also builds a trusted brand that users turn to, knowing that they will find valuable content that meets their needs.

In essence, the dynamic process of understanding and adapting to user intent and behaviour is what helps me sustain a successful digital presence. It empowers me to not just meet but anticipate the needs of my audience, positioning me to effectively guide them from initial curiosity to loyal advocacy. This is not just SEO; it's a strategic, user-focused approach that drives everything I do in the digital space. Let's look at an example…

Increasing Conversion Rates by 70% for a Major Insurance Client

When a pretty big insurance company approached me for SEO assistance, they were grappling with low conversion rates despite attracting substantial traffic. My initial audit revealed several critical issues: their website content was not aligned with user intent, and they had not thoroughly understood their target audience's behaviours and preferences. To address these challenges and ultimately achieve a 70% increase in conversion rates, I developed a strategy that involved understanding their target demographics deeply and tailoring content to meet user behaviour and preferences.

Initial Observations and Strategy Development

Upon taking on the insurance client, the first task was to understand their target demographics comprehensively. Using tools like Google Analytics and Google Search Console, I gathered data on visitor behaviour, identifying which content users were engaging with and the keywords driving traffic. This analysis revealed that a significant portion of their audience was searching for specific types of insurance coverage, indicating strong informational and commercial investigation intents.

To gain deeper insights, I conducted comprehensive audience research using social media insights, customer surveys, and feedback forms. This research helped develop detailed psychographic profiles, revealing key insights into the values, preferences, and pain points of potential customers. For example, many users were concerned about the affordability and comprehensiveness of insurance coverage, and they valued clear, jargon-free explanations.

Armed with this information, I refined the SEO strategy to align with the audience's search behaviours and preferences. Keyword research was tailored to reflect the specific language and queries used by the target demographics. Instead of focusing on broad, highly competitive terms, we targeted long-tail keywords that were more specific to user needs, such as "affordable car insurance for families" and "comprehensive home insurance quotes."

Tailoring the SEO and Content Strategy

Content customisation was crucial to addressing the audience's needs and improving conversion rates. I collaborated with the client's content team to create high-quality, informative articles and guides that answered common questions and concerns about insurance. This content was crafted in a clear, accessible tone, avoiding industry jargon that could alienate potential customers. Additionally, we developed comparison charts and FAQs to help users make informed decisions.

To further engage users, we created interactive content such as insurance calculators and quizzes that helped users determine their insurance needs. These tools not only provided value but also captured user information for follow-up marketing efforts.

Incorporating user-generated content, such as testimonials and case studies, was another strategy we employed. This type of content added credibility and helped build trust with potential customers. By showcasing real-life experiences and success stories, we demonstrated the benefits and reliability of the insurance products.

Optimising Marketing Channels

Knowing where the target audience spent their time online guided our marketing efforts. We leveraged platforms like LinkedIn and Facebook to reach professional and family-oriented demographics with tailored content and ads. On LinkedIn, we shared informative articles and industry insights that resonated with professionals looking for reliable insurance options. On Facebook, we used targeted ads to reach families and individuals, promoting content that addressed common insurance concerns.

We also focused on email marketing to nurture leads generated from our interactive tools. Personalised email campaigns provided tailored recommendations and follow-up information, keeping potential customers engaged and moving them further down the conversion funnel. By segmenting the email list based on user behaviour and preferences, we ensured that each email was relevant and valuable to the recipient.

Continuous monitoring and adjustment were key to our approach. Using analytics tools, we tracked the performance of our content and campaigns, making data-driven adjustments to optimise results. We paid close attention to metrics like click-through rates, bounce rates, and conversion rates to ensure our strategies were effective. For example, if a particular piece of content was not performing well, we analysed the data to understand why and made necessary adjustments to improve engagement.

Results and Impact

This all paid off. Within six months, this insurance client saw a 70% increase in conversion rates. Our targeted content and keyword strategies ensured that this traffic was highly relevant, addressing the specific needs and intents of the audience.

The use of interactive tools and personalised follow-up campaigns further enhanced user engagement and conversion. By focusing on the specific behaviours and preferences of their target demographics, we created a user experience that was not only informative but also highly engaging and trustworthy.

For instance, the interactive insurance calculators were particularly successful. Users appreciated the ability to input their specific circumstances and receive tailored insurance recommendations. This personalised approach helped to build trust and demonstrate the value of the insurance products, leading to higher conversion rates.

This approach highlights the transformative impact of understanding and targeting audience demographics, addressing technical SEO issues, and crafting a user-centric content strategy. By combining these elements, I was able to significantly improve the client's conversion rates and overall digital presence, demonstrating the power of a holistic, informed approach to SEO and digital marketing.

CHAPTER 4

TECHNICAL SEO

Technical SEO: Website Architecture

A well-structured URL is often the unsung hero of SEO, silently working in the background to enhance a website's visibility, user experience, and overall effectiveness. URLs, or Uniform Resource Locators, are the addresses of your web pages and serve as critical signals to search engines and users about the content and structure of your site. Let's delve into why well-structured URLs are crucial and how they can impact your SEO efforts.

Clarity and Relevance

At the heart of a well-structured URL is clarity and relevance. A clear, descriptive URL gives users and search engines a concise understanding of what to expect from the page. For example, a URL like "www.yoursite.com/seo-tips" immediately tells users that the page contains tips about SEO. This not only improves user experience but also helps search engines categorise and rank your content more effectively.

When URLs are concise and descriptive, they provide an instant snapshot of the page content, which can improve click-through rates from search engine results pages (SERPs). Users are more likely to click on a link that clearly matches their search intent. Additionally, URLs that reflect the page content accurately can reduce bounce rates, as users are more likely to find the information they were searching for, thus staying longer on your site.

SEO Keywords in URLs

Incorporating relevant keywords into your URLs can enhance SEO performance. While not as significant as they once were, keywords in URLs still send signals to search engines about the content and context of the page. For instance, if your page is about "digital marketing strategies," a URL like "www.yoursite.com/digital-marketing-strategies" is preferable over a generic or non-descriptive URL like "www.yoursite.com/page1."

Using keywords in URLs helps search engines understand the relevance of your page in relation to specific search queries. This can slightly boost your rankings for those keywords, making your content more discoverable to users searching for related terms. However, it's essential to avoid keyword stuffing, which can appear spammy and be penalised by search engines. Aim for natural, readable URLs that incorporate keywords in a meaningful way.

User Experience and Trust

User experience is paramount in SEO, and well-structured URLs contribute significantly to this. Clean, readable URLs are easier for users to remember and share, which can increase direct traffic and social sharing. URLs that are laden with complex strings of numbers and symbols can deter users from clicking on or sharing the link, reducing potential traffic and engagement.

A URL that looks clean and professional instils trust in users. It signals that your site is well-maintained and credible, which can encourage users to explore further. For example, compare "www.yoursite.com/seo-guide" with "www.yoursite.com/index.php?id=1234&session=5678". The former is much more likely to be trusted and clicked on.

Site Architecture and Navigation

URLs are integral to the overall architecture and navigation of your site. A well-structured URL hierarchy can help create a logical and organised site structure, making it easier for both users and search engines to navigate. For example, a structure like "www.yoursite.com/category/subcategory/page" clearly indicates the relationship between different levels of content and helps users understand where they are on the site.

A logical URL structure also aids in breadcrumb navigation, which enhances user experience by providing clear paths to navigate back to previous sections of the site. This can keep users engaged for longer periods, reducing bounce rates and increasing the likelihood of conversions.

Indexing and Crawling

For search engines, a well-structured URL is a roadmap that helps in efficient crawling and indexing of your site. When URLs are organised logically, search engine bots can crawl your site more effectively, ensuring that all important pages are discovered and indexed. This can lead to better overall visibility and improved rankings in search results.

Complex and disorganised URLs can create obstacles for search engine bots, potentially leading to issues with indexing. For example, URLs with excessive parameters or session IDs can cause duplicate content issues or crawl errors, which can negatively impact your SEO performance. Simplifying and organising your URLs helps prevent these issues and ensures that your site is fully accessible to search engines.

Best Practices for Well-Structured URLs

To maximise the benefits of well-structured URLs, here are some best practices to follow:

- Keep URLs Short and Descriptive: Aim for brevity while ensuring that the URL accurately describes the content of the page.
- Use Keywords Wisely: Include relevant keywords but avoid overstuffing. Make sure the URL remains readable and natural.

- Avoid Special Characters: Stick to hyphens to separate words and avoid underscores, spaces, and special characters.

- Use Lowercase Letters: URLs are case-sensitive, and using lowercase letters can prevent potential issues with duplicate content.

- Maintain a Logical Hierarchy: Reflect the structure of your site in your URLs to improve navigation and user understanding.

- Avoid Unnecessary Parameters: Simplify URLs by removing unnecessary parameters and keeping them clean.

Well-structured URLs are a fundamental component of effective SEO. They enhance user experience, improve search engine visibility, and contribute to a cohesive and navigable site architecture. By adhering to best practices and focusing on clarity, relevance, and simplicity, you can ensure that your URLs support your broader SEO objectives and drive better results for your website.

In an episode of Google's *Search Off The Record* podcast, Gary Illyes, an analyst at Google, highlighted a significant issue for search engine crawlers: URL parameters. This problem is particularly relevant for large or e-commerce websites that often use URL parameters to track, filter, and sort products, leading to an almost infinite number of URL variations for the same content.

Illyes explained that URL parameters can create what amounts to an infinite number of URLs for a single page. While these variations might lead to the same content, crawlers are unable to determine this without visiting each URL. This inefficiency in crawling can lead to wasted resources and potential indexing issues, making it harder for important pages to be crawled and indexed.

Historically, Google offered a URL Parameters tool in Search Console to help webmasters manage this issue by indicating which parameters were important and which could be ignored. However, this tool was deprecated in 2022, raising concerns among SEOs about how to handle the problem moving forward.

Illyes hinted at potential solutions that Google is exploring, including developing algorithms to better identify redundant URLs. He also suggested that clearer communication from website owners about their URL structure could help, and that the use of robots.txt files could be more effective in guiding crawlers.

The implications for SEO are significant, especially for large sites. Managing URL parameters is crucial for conserving crawl budget and ensuring that important pages are properly crawled and indexed. Developers might need to reconsider how they structure URLs, particularly in the context of faceted navigation on e-commerce sites. Additionally, the use of canonical tags can help Google understand which URL version should be treated as the primary one, further aiding in efficient crawling and indexing.

Site Hierarchy and Navigation

The structure of your website plays a crucial role in both user experience and SEO. A well-organised site hierarchy and intuitive navigation system make it easier for visitors to find what they're looking for and for search engines to crawl and index your content. This section will delve into the importance of site hierarchy, best practices for creating an effective navigation system, and the impact these elements have on your overall SEO strategy.

The Importance of Site Hierarchy

Site hierarchy refers to the way you organise your web pages and how they relate to each other. A logical, well-planned hierarchy helps users and search engines understand the structure of your site and the relationship between different pages. Here's why a good site hierarchy is essential:

Improved User Experience: A clear hierarchy ensures that users can easily find the information they need. When visitors can quickly navigate through your site, they are more likely to stay longer, explore more content, and ultimately convert into customers or subscribers.

Enhanced Crawlability: Search engine bots rely on your site's structure to navigate and index content. A well-defined hierarchy ensures that all important pages are accessible, reducing the risk of crawl errors and improving the chances of your pages being indexed.

Topic Distribution: A hierarchical structure allows you to strategically distribute topics across different levels of your site. This can help in targeting a broad range of search queries, improving your site's visibility for various things

Authority Distribution: Pages closer to the homepage are generally perceived as more important by search engines. A clear hierarchy helps distribute authority more effectively across your site, ensuring that high-priority pages receive the attention they deserve.

Best Practices for Creating an Effective Site Hierarchy

Creating an effective site hierarchy involves careful planning and organisation. Here are some best practices to guide you:

Start with a Clear Plan: Before you start building or reorganising your site, map out the structure. Identify your main categories and subcategories, and decide how your content will be organised within these sections.

Use a Logical Structure: Organise your content in a way that makes sense to your users. Typically, this involves a top-down approach, starting with broad categories that narrow down into more specific subcategories and pages. For example, an e-commerce site might start with broad categories like "Men's Clothing" and "Women's Clothing," which then narrow down to specific items like "Shirts" or "Pants."

Limit the Depth of Clicks: Ideally, users should be able to reach any page on your site within three to four clicks from the homepage. This not only improves user experience but also makes it easier for search engines to crawl your site efficiently.

Consistent Naming Conventions: Use clear and consistent naming conventions for your categories and pages. This helps users understand what each section is about and improves search engine indexing.

Use Breadcrumbs: Breadcrumbs are a secondary navigation system that shows users the path they have taken to reach a particular page. They enhance user experience by providing an easy way to navigate back to previous sections and help search engines understand the structure of your site.

Optimise Internal Linking: Use internal links to connect related content and help distribute link equity across your site. Internal links guide users to additional relevant content and help search engines discover and index all your pages.

Use a Flat Architecture When Possible: A flat site architecture means that all your important pages are just a few clicks away from the homepage. This is beneficial for both users and search engines, as it makes your content more accessible.

Navigation: The User's Guide to Your Site

Navigation is the system you use to help visitors find their way around your site. It includes elements like menus, links, and other interactive features. Effective navigation is critical for user experience and SEO because it directly impacts how easily users and search engines can access your content.

Primary Navigation Menu: This is the main menu that users see at the top of your site. It should include links to the most important sections of your site, like your main categories and key pages such as "About Us," "Contact," and "Services." Keep the menu simple and uncluttered to avoid overwhelming users.

Secondary Navigation: Secondary navigation menus can be used for less critical links that still need to be easily accessible. This might include links to your blog, FAQs, or policy pages. Place these menus in less prominent areas like the footer or a sidebar.

Mega Menus: For sites with a lot of content, a mega menu can be a useful tool. These expansive dropdown menus display multiple levels of navigation at once, allowing users to see a comprehensive overview of your site's structure. Ensure that mega menus are well-organised and easy to navigate.

Footer Navigation: The footer is a valuable area for navigation links. It's a good place for including links to important but less frequently accessed pages, such as legal disclaimers, privacy policies, and secondary sections of your site.

Search Functionality: A robust search function is essential, especially for larger sites. Ensure that your search bar is prominently placed and that it delivers relevant results. Consider implementing features like autocomplete and filters to enhance the search experience.

Mobile Navigation: With the increasing use of mobile devices, optimising your navigation for mobile is crucial. Use responsive design to ensure your navigation menus adapt well to smaller screens. Hamburger menus (those three-line icons) are commonly used for mobile navigation and can save space while still providing comprehensive access to your site's content.

Navigation Labels: Use clear, descriptive labels for your navigation links. Users should be able to understand what each link leads to at a glance. Avoid jargon or overly creative terms that might confuse visitors.

Interactive Elements: Make sure that interactive elements like dropdowns, tabs, and buttons are easy to use. Test them thoroughly to ensure they work well across different devices and browsers.

The Website Structure's Impact on SEO

A well-structured site hierarchy and intuitive navigation system can significantly enhance your SEO performance. Here's how:

Improved Crawl Efficiency: Search engines use crawlers to navigate your site and index its content. A clear, logical hierarchy and efficient navigation system ensure that crawlers can easily find and index all your important pages.

Enhanced User Experience: Positive user experience is a critical ranking factor. When users find your site easy to navigate, they are more likely to stay longer, engage with your content, and return in the future. This behaviour signals to search engines that your site is valuable and relevant.

Reduced Bounce Rates (or, higher Engagement Rates): Effective navigation helps users find what they're looking for quickly, reducing the likelihood that they will leave your site out of frustration. Lower bounce rates can improve your search rankings, as they indicate that your site meets user expectations.

Better Link Equity Distribution: Internal links within a well-structured hierarchy help distribute link equity across your site. This means that authority from high-value pages can flow to other important pages, boosting their visibility and ranking potential.

Context and Relevance: A clear site structure helps search engines understand the context and relevance of your content. This understanding can improve how your pages are indexed and ranked, particularly for complex queries.

Higher Conversion Rates: An intuitive navigation system makes it easier for users to find and interact with your content, leading to higher conversion rates. Whether it's making a purchase, signing up for a newsletter, or filling out a contact form, effective navigation can guide users smoothly through the conversion process.

A well-structured site hierarchy and intuitive navigation are foundational elements of effective SEO. They enhance user experience, improve crawl efficiency, and help distribute link equity across your site. By implementing best practices in these areas, you can create a website that is not only easy to navigate but also optimised for search engine visibility and performance.

Mobile-First Design and AMP

Optimising your website for mobile devices is no longer optional—it's essential. With the increasing prevalence of smartphones and tablets, more users are accessing the internet via mobile devices than ever before. This shift has profound implications for how websites should be designed and optimised. In this section, I'll explore the principles of mobile-first design and why it's crucial for SEO. I'll also discuss Accelerated Mobile Pages (AMP) and why, despite its initial promise, it may not be the best approach for ensuring fast loading times.

The Shift to Mobile-First Design

Mobile-first design prioritises the mobile user experience over the desktop experience. This approach involves designing your website for mobile devices first and then scaling up for larger screens. This paradigm shift reflects the reality that a significant portion of web traffic comes from mobile devices.

Mobile-first design is important for several reasons. Firstly, Google now uses mobile-first indexing, which means it primarily uses the mobile version of the content for indexing and ranking. If your mobile site is not optimised, your rankings on Google could suffer significantly. Secondly, mobile users expect a seamless, fast, and intuitive experience. If your site is difficult to navigate or slow to load on a mobile device, users are likely to bounce quickly and look for alternatives. Lastly, an optimised mobile experience can lead to higher engagement, more traffic, and increased conversions. Users are more likely to stay on your site and complete desired actions if their mobile experience is positive.

The principles of mobile-first design involve creating a responsive design that automatically adjusts to fit the screen sie of the device being used. Simplified navigation is crucial since mobile screens are smaller. Use hamburger menus, collapsible sections, and easily tappable buttons to make navigation intuitive. Fast loading times are essential as mobile users are often on the go and have less patience for slow-loading pages. Optimise images, use lay loading, and minimise JavaScript to enhance loading speeds. Design with touch interactions in mind by ensuring buttons and links are large enough to tap easily and that there is enough spacing between interactive elements to prevent accidental clicks. Prioritise the most important content and features for mobile users, hiding or moving less critical elements to secondary pages. Embrace minimalism by reducing clutter and focusing on essential elements, which improves aesthetics and enhances performance by reducing the amount of data that needs to be loaded.

Accelerated Mobile Pages (AMP)

Accelerated Mobile Pages (AMP) is an open-source framework designed to create fast-loading mobile pages. It was introduced by Google to improve the mobile web experience by simplifying HTML and allowing only certain JavaScript to run. While AMP initially gained traction for its potential to speed up mobile web performance, it has faced criticism and declining adoption in recent years.

AMP imposes strict limitations on how you can design and customise your pages, often resulting in a less dynamic and engaging user experience compared to fully optimised mobile pages built without AMP constraints. Maintaining separate versions of your site for AMP and non-AMP can be cumbersome and time-consuming, leading to inconsistencies and additional workload for your development team. Although AMP pages are often highlighted in Google's search results, the SEO benefits are not as significant as they once were. Google's shift towards overall page experience metrics, including Core Web Vitals, means that non-AMP pages can perform just as well if they are optimised for speed and usability. AMP's restrictive framework can sometimes lead to a suboptimal user experience. The limitations on interactivity and the forced use of simplified templates can make AMP pages feel less engaging. Advances in web technologies and optimisation techniques have made it possible to achieve fast loading times without AMP. Techniques such as lazy loading, efficient caching, and optimising server response times can create fast and responsive mobile pages without the need for AMP.

Creating fast-loading pages without AMP involves optimising images by using modern formats like WebP, compressing images without losing quality, and implementing responsive images to serve the right size based on the device. Minimise JavaScript by reducing the amount of JavaScript on your pages, deferring non-critical scripts, and eliminating unused code, which reduces load time and improves interactivity. Leverage browser caching by configuring your server to store static resources in the user's browser cache, ensuring that subsequent visits to your site will load faster as elements are loaded from the cache rather than the server. Use a Content Delivery Network (CDN) to distribute your content across multiple servers worldwide, ensuring that users access your site from the server closest to them, reducing load times. Implement lazy loading to defer the loading of non-critical resources until they are needed, significantly speeding up the initial load time of your pages. Optimise CSS delivery by minimising CSS files and using inline critical CSS to load essential styles quickly, preventing render-blocking and improving perceived load times. Improve server response time by optimising your server and database to respond faster to requests, which can be achieved through efficient coding practices, database indexing, and using a reliable hosting provider.

While AMP was once a popular solution for improving mobile page speed, its limitations and the availability of better alternatives make it less appealing today. Focusing on mobile-first design principles and implementing best practices for fast loading times can provide a superior user experience and SEO performance without the need for AMP. Embrace the shift to mobile-first design to ensure your website meets the expectations of modern users and search engines alike, positioning your site for success in the increasingly mobile-centric digital landscape.

Speed and Performance Optimisation

At the time of writing this In 2024, the importance of speed and performance optimisation for SEO has never been more pronounced. At the forefront of this movement is Google's Core Web Vitals, a set of specific factors that Google considers essential in a webpage's overall user experience. These metrics, alongside other user experience metrics, are crucial for determining how well your site performs and ranks in search engine results.

Understanding Core Web Vitals

Core Web Vitals consist of three primary metrics: Largest Contentful Paint (LCP), First Input Delay (FID), and Cumulative Layout Shift (CLS). Each of these metrics addresses a different aspect of the user experience, focusing on load performance, interactivity, and visual stability.

Largest Contentful Paint (LCP)

LCP measures the time it takes for the largest content element on a page to become visible within the viewport. This could be an image, video, or a large block of text. Ideally, LCP should occur within 2.5 seconds of when the page first starts loading. A fast LCP reassures users that the page is loading efficiently and content is quickly accessible.

First Input Delay (FID)

FID measures the time from when a user first interacts with your page (clicking a link, tapping a button, etc.) to when the browser responds to that interaction. An ideal FID is less than 100 milliseconds. A low FID ensures that the page is not only visually complete but also ready for user interaction, enhancing the overall user experience.

Cumulative Layout Shift (CLS)

CLS measures the sum total of all unexpected layout shifts that occur during the entire lifespan of the page. An ideal CLS score is less than 0.1. This metric ensures that elements on the page do not move around unexpectedly, which can be a source of frustration for users trying to interact with the content.

The Importance of Core Web Vitals

Core Web Vitals are critical for several reasons. Firstly, they directly impact user satisfaction. Users are likely to abandon a site that loads slowly, is unresponsive, or shifts content unexpectedly. Secondly, these metrics are now a significant part of Google's ranking algorithm.

Google uses Core Web Vitals as part of its Page Experience update to rank pages based on the quality of user experience they provide. Thus, optimising for these metrics can improve both user satisfaction and search engine rankings.

Other User Experience Metrics

While Core Web Vitals are essential, they are part of a broader set of user experience metrics that webmasters should pay attention to. These include metrics like Time to First Byte (TTFB), Speed Index, and Time to Interactive (TTI).

Time to First Byte (TTFB)

TTFB measures the time it takes for a user's browser to receive the first byte of page content from the server. A lower TTFB means that the server is responding quickly, which is crucial for fast page load times. Optimising server performance, using a Content Delivery Network (CDN), and improving backend efficiency can help reduce TTFB.

Speed Index

Speed Index shows how quickly the content of a page is visibly populated. It is a measure of how quickly users perceive that the page is loading. A lower Speed Index indicates that the page content is rendering quickly, contributing to a better user experience.

Time to Interactive (TTI)

TTI measures how long it takes for a page to become fully interactive. It is the point at which a page appears visually complete and can reliably respond to user interactions. A lower TTI enhances the user's ability to interact with the page promptly, improving overall user satisfaction.

Strategies for Optimising Core Web Vitals and User Experience Metrics

To optimise Core Web Vitals and other user experience metrics, a multifaceted approach is necessary. Here are some strategies that can help:

Optimise Images and Media: Large images and media files can significantly slow down LCP. Use next-gen image formats like WebP, compress images without losing quality, and implement responsive images to ensure they load quickly on all device types.

Minimise JavaScript: Heavy JavaScript can delay interactivity and contribute to high FID and TTI. Minimise JavaScript, defer non-essential scripts, and use techniques like code splitting to improve load times.

Implement Lazy Loading: Lazy loading defers the loading of non-critical resources until they are needed. This reduces initial load times and improves LCP and Speed Index.

Enhance Server Response Times: Improve your server performance by optimising backend processes, using efficient database queries, and leveraging server-side caching. A faster server response time reduces TTFB and improves overall page load times.

Use Content Delivery Networks (CDNs): CDNs distribute your content across multiple servers worldwide, ensuring that users access your site from the server closest to them. This can drastically reduce load times and improve all Core Web Vitals.

Avoid Layout Shifts: Ensure that elements on your page have reserved spaces to prevent unexpected shifts. Use CSS aspect ratio boxes for images and videos, and avoid inserting dynamic content above existing content without a placeholder.

Prioritise Critical CSS: Load critical CSS inline to ensure it is available immediately. Defer non-critical CSS to prevent render-blocking issues that can delay LCP and TTI.

Monitor and Adjust: Regularly monitor your site's performance using tools like Google PageSpeed Insights, Lighthouse, and Search Console. Continuously test and refine your optimisations to keep up with changes in user behaviour and search engine algorithms.

The emphasis on Core Web Vitals and user experience metrics underscores the growing importance of delivering a fast, responsive, and visually stable web experience. By prioritising these metrics, you can enhance user satisfaction, improve your SEO performance, and stay ahead.

Tools for Speed Testing and Monitoring

Understanding the performance of your website is essential for optimising speed and ensuring a positive user experience. Numerous tools are available to help you test and monitor the speed and performance of your site. These tools provide insights into how quickly your site loads, identifies areas for improvement, and track performance over time.

One of the most popular tools for speed testing is **Google PageSpeed Insights**. This tool analyses your site's performance on both mobile and desktop devices, providing detailed suggestions for improvement. It evaluates various metrics, including First Contentful Paint (FCP), Largest Contentful Paint (LCP), and Cumulative Layout Shift (CLS), which are essential for understanding your Core Web Vitals. PageSpeed Insights also offers practical recommendations, such as image optimisation, script minimisation, and server response time improvements.

Another valuable tool is **Google Lighthouse**. This open-source, automated tool audits your website's performance, accessibility, SEO, and more. Lighthouse provides a comprehensive report with actionable insights, helping you understand the specific elements that may be slowing down your site. By integrating Lighthouse with your development workflow, you can ensure ongoing performance improvements and maintain a high-quality user experience.

GTmetrix is another excellent tool for evaluating website performance. It offers detailed reports on various performance metrics, including page load time, total page size, and the number of requests. GTmetrix also provides recommendations for optimisation, such as leveraging browser caching, optimising images, and reducing server response time. Its waterfall chart visualisation helps you understand the sequence and duration of each request made by your site, making it easier to identify bottlenecks.

Pingdom is a widely-used tool for monitoring website performance and uptime. It offers real-time insights into how your site performs across different locations and devices. Pingdom's detailed reports highlight areas that need attention, such as slow-loading elements and long server response times. With its continuous monitoring capabilities, Pingdom alerts you to any performance issues as they arise, allowing you to address them promptly and maintain optimal site performance.

WebPageTest is a powerful tool that provides in-depth performance testing from multiple locations worldwide. It offers a range of advanced testing features, including video capture, content blocking, and multi-step transactions. WebPageTest's detailed reports include metrics such as Time to First Byte (TTFB), Start Render, and Speed Index, helping you pinpoint performance issues and understand how different factors impact your site's load time.

For those looking to monitor performance over time, **New Relic** offers comprehensive performance monitoring and analytics. This tool provides real-time insights into your site's performance, including server response times, database queries, and application performance. New Relic's dashboards and alerts help you stay on top of performance trends, identify potential issues before they impact users, and make data-driven decisions to enhance your site's speed and reliability.

Another essential tool is the **Chrome DevTools**, a set of web developer tools built directly into the Google Chrome browser. DevTools allows you to inspect network activity, analyse page load performance, and diagnose rendering issues. Its Performance panel provides a detailed timeline of your page's loading process, highlighting areas where optimisations can be made. By using DevTools, you can gain a deeper understanding of how your site behaves in real-time and make informed adjustments to improve performance.

Additionally, **Google Search Console** offers valuable insights into how your site performs in Google's search results. It includes a Core Web Vitals report that highlights pages with performance issues related to LCP, FID, and CLS. By regularly reviewing this report, you can identify and address performance problems that may be affecting your site's search rankings and user experience.

Regularly using these tools to test and monitor your site's speed and performance is crucial for maintaining a high-quality user experience and optimising your SEO efforts. By understanding the specific factors that impact your site's performance and implementing the recommended improvements, you can ensure that your website remains fast, responsive, and competitive in the ever-evolving digital landscape.

Strategies for Performance Improvement

This part might get a bit boring for those of you who don't want to get into too much technical detail. But I can't leave it out.

Improving your website's performance is a multifaceted endeavour that requires a strategic approach. While we have touched on some methods already, such as optimising images and minimising JavaScript, this section will delve deeper into comprehensive strategies that can significantly enhance your site's speed and overall user experience.

A critical first step in performance improvement is optimising your images and media. Images are often the largest assets on a web page and can significantly impact load times if not properly managed. Use modern image formats like WebP, which offer superior compression and quality compared to traditional formats. Compress images to reduce their file size without compromising quality. Implement responsive images to serve appropriately sized images based on the user's device, ensuring that mobile users are not downloading unnecessarily large files. Additionally, consider using lazy loading for images and videos. Lazy loading defers the loading of non-essential resources until they are needed, reducing the initial load time and making your site appear faster to users.

JavaScript is another area where optimisation can lead to substantial performance gains. Heavy JavaScript can delay interactivity and increase page load times. Minimise the amount of JavaScript on your pages by removing unused code and deferring non-critical scripts. Consider using code-splitting techniques, which break down large JavaScript files into smaller, more manageable chunks that can be loaded as needed. By reducing the JavaScript footprint, you can improve metrics such as First Input Delay (FID) and Time to Interactive (TTI), enhancing the overall user experience.

Server response times play a pivotal role in how quickly your site loads. Enhancing server performance involves optimising backend processes and ensuring efficient database queries. Leveraging server-side caching can significantly reduce the time it takes to generate pages dynamically. Utilise a Content Delivery Network (CDN) to distribute your content across multiple servers worldwide. CDNs ensure that users access your site from the server closest to them, drastically reducing load times and improving performance for a global audience.

CSS optimisation is another crucial factor in improving site performance. Minimise CSS files and prioritise loading critical CSS inline to ensure essential styles are available immediately. This prevents render-blocking issues, where the browser must load and parse CSS files before rendering the page. By streamlining CSS delivery, you can enhance metrics like Largest Contentful Paint (LCP) and Speed Index, ensuring that your pages load swiftly and smoothly.

Another effective strategy for performance improvement is leveraging browser caching. Configuring your server to store static resources in the user's browser cache can drastically reduce load times on subsequent visits. This means that elements such as images, stylesheets, and scripts are loaded from the cache rather than being fetched from the server each time, providing a faster and more seamless user experience.

Regularly monitoring and refining your performance strategies is essential. Use tools like Google PageSpeed Insights, Lighthouse, and GTmetrix to track your site's performance over time and identify areas for improvement. These tools offer actionable insights and recommendations that can help you fine-tune your optimisations and stay ahead of performance issues.

Addressing layout shifts is also vital for improving user experience. Cumulative Layout Shift (CLS) measures the unexpected movement of web elements during the loading process. Ensuring that elements on your page have reserved spaces can prevent unexpected shifts. Use CSS aspect ratio boxes for images and videos and avoid inserting dynamic content above existing content without a placeholder. This approach will help maintain visual stability and improve user satisfaction.

Lastly, it is crucial to keep an eye on evolving web standards and best practices. The web development landscape is constantly changing, with new technologies and techniques emerging regularly. Stay informed about the latest developments and be ready to adapt your strategies accordingly. Engaging with the web development community, attending conferences, and participating in online forums can provide valuable insights and keep you updated on the latest trends and best practices.

Improving website performance is an ongoing process that requires a holistic approach. By focusing on optimising images and media, minimising JavaScript, enhancing server response times, optimising CSS, leveraging browser caching, addressing layout shifts, and staying updated with industry developments, you can ensure that your site delivers a fast, responsive, and enjoyable experience for users. These strategies, when implemented consistently, will not only enhance user satisfaction but also improve your search engine rankings and overall digital presence.

Headless CMS

A headless CMS (Content Management System) is a modern approach to managing and delivering content that separates the backend (where content is created and managed) from the frontend (where content is presented to users). Unlike traditional CMSs, where the content, presentation, and business logic are tightly coupled, a headless CMS allows developers to choose their own front-end frameworks and technologies to deliver content via APIs. This flexibility can significantly enhance page speed and overall website performance, but it's important to consider the potential drawbacks as well.

Benefits for Page Speed

One of the primary benefits of using a headless CMS is the improvement in page speed, which is crucial for both user experience and SEO performance. A headless CMS delivers content via APIs, which means that the content can be fetched asynchronously and loaded in parallel with other resources on the page. This results in faster initial load times and a more responsive user experience.

Additionally, a headless CMS allows developers to optimise the frontend independently of the backend, enabling the use of modern web technologies such as React, Angular, or Vue.js. These frameworks are designed for fast rendering and can significantly reduce the time it takes for a page to become interactive. The decoupled nature of a headless CMS also means that unnecessary backend processes do not interfere with the frontend performance, further enhancing page speed.

Another advantage is the ability to implement content delivery networks (CDNs) more effectively. Since a headless CMS serves content via APIs, it can be easily integrated with CDNs, which cache content closer to the user, reducing latency and improving load times globally. This is particularly beneficial for websites with a large, geographically dispersed audience.

Drawbacks of Using a Headless CMS

While the benefits of a headless CMS for page speed are significant, there are also several drawbacks that need to be considered. One of the main challenges is the complexity of implementation and maintenance. A headless CMS requires a higher level of technical expertise compared to traditional CMSs. Developers must be proficient in front-end technologies and API integration, which can increase development time and costs.

Another drawback is the potential for fragmented workflows. In a traditional CMS, content creation, management, and presentation are handled within a single system. With a headless CMS, content creators and developers often work in separate environments, which can lead to communication gaps and inefficiencies. Additionally, the lack of a visual editor in some headless CMSs means that content creators may need to rely on developers to preview how content will look on the frontend, which can slow down the content production process.

SEO challenges can also arise with a headless CMS. While the flexibility of a headless approach allows for better optimisation, it also requires more effort to ensure that SEO best practices are followed. For instance, implementing meta tags, structured data, and canonical URLs may require custom development, as opposed to being built-in features of a traditional CMS. Moreover, because headless CMSs often rely on JavaScript frameworks for rendering, care must be taken to ensure that search engines can crawl and index the content effectively.

Another consideration is the cost of transitioning to a headless CMS. Migrating from a traditional CMS to a headless architecture can be resource-intensive, involving both time and money. Additionally, because headless CMSs are often priced based on API calls and content delivery, costs can scale quickly as the website grows, which might be a concern for businesses with limited budgets.

Lastly, while a headless CMS offers flexibility, it can also lead to a lack of standardised tools and practices. Unlike traditional CMSs that come with built-in features and plugins, a headless CMS requires custom development for many common functionalities, which can lead to inconsistencies in how different parts of the website are built and maintained. This can make troubleshooting and updates more complicated and time-consuming.

In summary, while a headless CMS offers substantial benefits for page speed and overall website performance, particularly in terms of flexibility and modern web practices, it also introduces complexities that need to be carefully managed. The decision to adopt a headless CMS should be based on a thorough assessment of your technical capabilities, project requirements, and long-term maintenance resources.

HTTPS and Website Security

In the realm of technical SEO, website security is a critical factor that not only protects your site and its users but also influences your search engine rankings. One of the most fundamental aspects of website security is the use of HTTPS, a protocol that ensures secure communication over a computer network. As we delve into this topic, we will explore why HTTPS is essential, how it impacts SEO, and best practices for implementing it on your site.

The Importance of HTTPS

HTTPS stands for HyperText Transfer Protocol Secure. Unlike HTTP, which transfers data in plain text, HTTPS encrypts data between the user's browser and the server using the Secure Sockets Layer (SSL) or Transport Layer Security (TLS) protocols. This encryption protects sensitive information, such as passwords, credit card numbers, and personal data, from being intercepted by malicious actors.

The significance of HTTPS extends beyond data protection. Google has made it clear that HTTPS is a ranking factor. Websites using HTTPS are given a slight ranking boost compared to those still on HTTP. This is part of Google's broader initiative to promote a safer internet. Chrome, the most popular web browser, flags non-HTTPS sites as "Not Secure," which can deter users from visiting and engaging with your site. Thus, HTTPS is not only a security measure but also a crucial component of building trust with your audience and maintaining a professional online presence.

SEO Benefits of HTTPS

The transition to HTTPS offers several SEO benefits. Firstly, as mentioned, Google uses HTTPS as a ranking signal. While the boost may be modest, it can still provide an edge over competitors who have not yet made the switch. Moreover, HTTPS protects the integrity of your site by preventing tampering by third parties. This ensures that the content users see is the content you intended to deliver, free from malicious modifications.

HTTPS also plays a role in referral data. When traffic passes from an HTTPS site to an HTTP site, referral data is stripped away, making it appear as "direct" traffic in analytics. By using HTTPS, you preserve this referral data, giving you more accurate insights into where your traffic is coming from and how users are interacting with your site.

Implementing HTTPS

Transitioning your site from HTTP to HTTPS involves several steps, but the benefits far outweigh the initial effort. The first step is to obtain an SSL/TLS certificate from a trusted Certificate Authority (CA). These certificates come in various types, including Domain Validated (DV), Organisation Validated (OV), and Extended Validation (EV), each offering different levels of validation and trust indicators.

Once you have obtained and installed the SSL/TLS certificate on your server, you need to configure your website to use HTTPS. This involves updating your server settings to enforce HTTPS, ensuring that all internal links and resources (such as images, scripts, and stylesheets) are served over HTTPS, and setting up 301 redirects from HTTP to HTTPS to preserve your SEO equity and ensure a smooth transition for users.

It is also crucial to update your sitemap to reflect the new HTTPS URLs and resubmit it to search engines via Google Search Console and Bing Webmaster Tools. This helps search engines re-index your site more quickly and reduces the potential for indexing issues.

Best Practices for HTTPS Implementation

To maximise the benefits of HTTPS and avoid common pitfalls, follow these best practices. Ensure that your SSL/TLS certificate is up to date and does not expire. An expired certificate can lead to security warnings and loss of trust among users. Regularly monitor your site for mixed content issues, which occur when some elements on a page are still served over HTTP. Mixed content can undermine the security of your site and trigger browser warnings.

Use HTTP Strict Transport Security (HSTS) to enforce HTTPS across your site. HSTS tells browsers to only interact with your site over HTTPS, even if users attempt to access it via HTTP. This adds an additional layer of security by preventing protocol downgrade attacks and cookie hijacking.

Regularly test your site's security using tools like SSL Labs' SSL Test, which can identify potential vulnerabilities and areas for improvement. Keeping your server software and security certificates up to date is essential for maintaining robust security standards.

The Broader Impact of HTTPS on User Trust and Engagement

Beyond its technical and SEO advantages, HTTPS plays a significant role in user trust and engagement. In an age where data breaches and cyber threats are common, users are increasingly aware of the importance of online security. The presence of HTTPS, indicated by a padlock icon in the browser address bar, provides a visual assurance to users that their data is secure. This can lead to higher engagement rates, as users feel more confident in interacting with your site, sharing personal information, and completing transactions.

Moreover, sites that handle sensitive information, such as e-commerce platforms and financial services, must use HTTPS to comply with industry standards and regulations. Non-compliance can result in penalties and a loss of business. Therefore, HTTPS is not just a technical requirement but a critical element of your business strategy.

HTTPS is a cornerstone of modern website security and an essential factor in SEO. By securing the data transmitted between users and your site, building trust with your audience, and benefiting from enhanced search rankings, HTTPS offers comprehensive advantages. Implementing HTTPS is a strategic move that protects your users, strengthens your SEO efforts, and positions your site as a trustworthy and reliable destination in the digital landscape.

Safe Browsing and Penalties

In the digital landscape, maintaining a secure website is paramount not only for protecting your users but also for safeguarding your search engine rankings. Safe browsing involves creating an environment where users can navigate your site without encountering security threats such as malware, phishing, or harmful downloads. Search engines, particularly Google, are vigilant in promoting safe browsing and penalising sites that pose risks to users. This section will explore the importance of safe browsing, the types of penalties associated with security breaches, and strategies to avoid them.

The Importance of Safe Browsing

Safe browsing is essential for maintaining user trust and engagement. When users visit your site, they expect a secure and seamless experience. Any indication of a security threat can lead to immediate disengagement, a drop in traffic, and lasting damage to your brand reputation. Beyond user perception, search engines have stringent measures to ensure that users are directed to safe and trustworthy sites. Google Safe Browsing, for instance, continuously scans websites for potential security threats. If a site is flagged, it can lead to significant penalties, including warnings displayed in search results and browsers, which can drastically reduce traffic and credibility.

Ensuring safe browsing involves several proactive measures. Regularly scanning your site for malware, implementing robust security protocols, and staying updated on the latest security threats are fundamental practices. Using services like Google Search Console to monitor your site's security status can help detect issues early. Immediate action in response to security alerts is crucial to mitigate risks and maintain a safe browsing environment.

Understanding Penalties for Security Breaches

When it comes to website security, the consequences of negligence can be severe. Search engines impose penalties on sites that are compromised or fail to adhere to security best practices. These penalties can range from reduced search rankings to complete removal from search results. The most common types of security-related penalties include:

Manual Actions: These are penalties manually applied by search engine reviewers. They can occur when your site is found to violate search engine guidelines, such as hosting malware, phishing content, or being involved in spammy practices. Manual actions result in lower rankings or removal from search results until the issues are resolved.

Algorithmic Penalties: These are automated penalties triggered by search engine algorithms when security issues are detected. For example, Google's Safe Browsing algorithm can automatically flag sites that distribute malware or engage in deceptive practices. These penalties often result in warning messages being displayed to users before they can access the site.

Browser Warnings: Browsers like Google Chrome and Mozilla Firefox use Safe Browsing to protect users. If your site is detected as unsafe, browsers will display warning pages to users, advising them to avoid your site. These warnings can severely impact traffic and user trust.

Strategies to Maintain Safe Browsing

Maintaining a secure site and avoiding penalties requires a proactive and ongoing approach. Here are several strategies to ensure safe browsing and protect your site from penalties:

Regularly updating your website's software and plugins is critical. Outdated software can have vulnerabilities that hackers exploit to gain unauthorised access. Implementing a robust update protocol ensures that your site benefits from the latest security patches and improvements.

Conducting regular security audits and scans helps identify potential vulnerabilities and threats. Use tools like Google Search Console, Sucuri SiteCheck, and other malware scanning services to perform comprehensive security checks. These tools can detect issues early, allowing you to address them before they become serious problems.

Implementing strong access controls is another essential strategy. Limit the number of individuals with administrative access to your site and enforce strong password policies. Two-factor authentication (2FA) adds an extra layer of security, making it harder for unauthorised users to gain access.

Regular backups of your site are crucial. In the event of a security breach, having recent backups ensures that you can quickly restore your site to a secure state. Automated backup solutions can help maintain regular and reliable backup routines.

Using a Web Application Firewall (WAF) can protect your site from various threats, including SQL injection, cross-site scripting (XSS), and distributed denial-of-service (DDoS) attacks. A WAF monitors and filters incoming traffic, blocking malicious activity before it reaches your site.

Ensuring secure data transmission is vital. HTTPS, as discussed in the previous section, encrypts data between the user's browser and your server, protecting it from interception. Additionally, make sure your website adheres to data protection regulations such as GDPR, which mandate secure handling and storage of personal data.

Monitoring user-generated content is also important. User-generated content, such as comments or forum posts, can be a vector for malware distribution if not properly moderated. Implementing moderation tools and automated filters can help keep user-generated content safe.

Staying informed about the latest security threats and trends is essential. The cybersecurity landscape is constantly evolving, and new threats emerge regularly. Engaging with cybersecurity communities, subscribing to security bulletins, and attending relevant webinars and conferences can keep you updated on the latest developments.

Responding to Security Incidents

Despite your best efforts, security incidents can still occur. How you respond to these incidents can significantly impact your site's recovery and reputation. Prompt action is crucial. As soon as a security issue is detected, take your site offline if necessary to prevent further damage. Conduct a thorough investigation to identify the cause and scope of the breach. Once the issue is identified, implement corrective measures to secure your site.

Communicating with your users is also important. Transparency can help maintain trust. Inform your users about the breach, the steps you are taking to address it, and any actions they should take, such as changing passwords.

After resolving the issue, request a review from search engines if you have received a manual action. Google Search Console provides a mechanism for site owners to request a review once the security issue has been fixed. Provide detailed information about the steps you have taken to resolve the issue and prevent future occurrences.

Maintaining a secure website is a continuous process that requires vigilance and proactive management. By prioritising safe browsing and adhering to security best practices, you can protect your users, avoid penalties, and ensure a positive user experience. This commitment to security not only enhances your SEO efforts but also builds trust and credibility with your audience, positioning your site as a reliable and trustworthy resource in the digital landscape.

Transforming a Retailer's SEO Through Security and Strategy

Once, when an Irish retailer approached me for SEO services, they were facing significant challenges that were undermining their online presence. Their website was not using HTTPS, which was affecting user trust and search engine rankings. To make matters worse, they had received a manual Google penalty due to security vulnerabilities that had resulted in their site being flagged for distributing malware. This situation was dire, but it also presented an opportunity to make impactful changes that could transform their online performance.

Identifying the Problems

During our initial audit, several critical issues stood out. The most glaring was the lack of HTTPS, which not only exposed the site to potential security threats but also displayed a "Not Secure" warning to visitors using browsers like Google Chrome. This warning was undoubtedly driving potential customers away and eroding trust in the brand.

Additionally, the site had received a manual penalty from Google. This was confirmed through Google Search Console, where I noticed a message indicating that the site had been flagged for hosting malicious content. The penalty had caused a significant drop in organic traffic and visibility, which was detrimental to the retailer's business.

Implementing HTTPS

The first step in our recovery plan was to secure the website by implementing HTTPS. I coordinated with the retailer's IT team to obtain an SSL/TLS certificate from a trusted Certificate Authority (CA). Given the urgency, we opted for an Extended Validation (EV) certificate, which not only provides robust encryption but also displays a green address bar in browsers, signalling to users that the site is secure and verified.

Once the certificate was installed, we updated the server settings to enforce HTTPS across the entire site. This included configuring the server to redirect all HTTP traffic to HTTPS using 301 redirects. We also ensured that all internal links, images, scripts, and stylesheets were served over HTTPS to prevent mixed content issues.

Addressing the Manual Penalty

With the site now secure, the next step was to address the manual penalty. I conducted a thorough security audit to identify and remove any malicious content that had been injected into the site. This involved scanning for malware, cleaning infected files, and patching any vulnerabilities that could be exploited in the future.

After cleaning the site, I prepared a detailed reconsideration request to Google. This request outlined the steps we had taken to secure the site, remove malicious content, and prevent future breaches. Transparency and detail were key in this request, as it demonstrated our commitment to maintaining a secure and trustworthy website.

Rebuilding Trust and Traffic

While waiting for Google to process the reconsideration request, we focused on rebuilding user trust and improving the overall user experience. This included updating the website's design to make it more user-friendly and engaging. We enhanced navigation, improved load times by optimising images and minimising JavaScript, and ensured that the site was mobile-friendly.

We also launched a content marketing campaign (more about this later!) to re-engage the retailer's audience. This involved creating high-quality, informative content tailored to the interests and needs of their target demographics. By leveraging the retailer's unique selling points and industry expertise, we aimed to rebuild authority and drive organic traffic.

Results and Recovery

After a few weeks, we received confirmation from Google that the manual penalty had been lifted. This marked a turning point for the retailer's online presence. With the penalty removed and the site now secure with HTTPS, we began to see a gradual increase in organic traffic and search engine rankings.

The retailer's customers responded positively to the changes. The "Not Secure" warnings were gone, and the presence of the green address bar in browsers instilled confidence. Our content marketing efforts also paid off, as we saw improved engagement metrics, longer session durations, and higher conversion rates.

Clearly, transforming the SEO performance of this Irish retailer was a challenging but rewarding experience. By prioritising security and addressing the critical issues head-on, we not only restored their search engine rankings but also rebuilt user trust and engagement. This case underscores the importance of a holistic approach to SEO, where technical optimisations, security measures, and quality content all play integral roles in achieving long-term success.

CHAPTER 5
ADVANCED DATA STRUCTURING

Structured data and schema markup play crucial roles in modern SEO strategies, offering multifaceted advantages that significantly impact a website's visibility, click-through rates (CTR), and overall search engine understanding. These tools not only enhance a site's search presence but also ensure that its content is accurately represented and readily discoverable by search engines and users alike.

At its core, structured data refers to a standardised format utilised for providing precise information about a webpage and categorising its content. By employing structured data, website owners empower search engines to better comprehend the substance of their pages, ultimately improving how these pages are depicted and ranked within search engine results. This alignment with search engine algorithms is fundamental to SEO success, as it directly influences a webpage's visibility and its potential for attracting organic traffic.

One of the most prevalent forms of structured data is schema markup. This markup language operates as a vocabulary of tags, commonly referred to as microdata, seamlessly integrated into the HTML code of a webpage. Through schema markup, webmasters can augment the manner in which search engines interpret and display their page content in Search Engine Results Pages (SERPs). This standardised approach to markup is made possible by Schema.org, a collaborative initiative that furnishes a comprehensive array of shared vocabularies. These vocabularies are recognised and employed by major search providers, including Google, Bing, and Yahoo, thereby ensuring compatibility and efficacy across diverse search platforms.

The implementation of structured data on a website can yield a myriad of benefits, with one of the most notable being the generation of rich snippets in search results. Rich snippets are enriched search listings that may incorporate various additional elements such as images, star ratings, prices, and other pertinent information directly within the search results. By presenting users with a more comprehensive preview of the webpage's content, rich snippets significantly enhance the visibility and appeal of the listing, consequently augmenting the likelihood of user engagement and click-through.

In essence, structured data and schema markup serve as indispensable tools in the modern SEO landscape, facilitating enhanced search engine comprehension, improved search result presentation, and ultimately, greater user engagement. Through strategic implementation and optimisation of structured data, website owners can unlock a wealth of opportunities to elevate their online visibility and drive sustainable organic traffic to their web properties.

Importance of Structured Data and Schema Markup

Structured data and schema markup represent indispensable components of contemporary SEO strategies, offering a multitude of benefits that extend far beyond mere visibility enhancements. Through the strategic implementation and optimisation of structured data, website owners can unlock a wealth of opportunities to elevate their online presence, drive organic traffic, and enhance user engagement across diverse search platforms.

Enhanced Visibility in SERPs: Structured data plays a pivotal role in augmenting a website's visibility within Search Engine Results Pages (SERPs). By leveraging schema markup, webmasters empower search engines to generate rich snippets that prominently showcase additional information directly within the search results. These rich snippets encompass a diverse array of elements, including images, product prices, ratings, and more, effectively distinguishing the website's listings from its competitors. As a result, users are more inclined to click on results that offer comprehensive previews of the content, thereby amplifying the website's overall visibility and click-through rates (CTR).

Improved Click-Through Rates (CTR): The implementation of structured data and the subsequent creation of rich snippets have been correlated with heightened click-through rates (CTR) for website listings. Users are naturally drawn to search results that provide supplementary and pertinent information directly within the SERPs. This is particularly advantageous for e-commerce websites, recipe pages, event listings, and review platforms, where rich snippets can furnish users with essential details at a glance, prompting them to click through to the website for further exploration and engagement.

Enhanced Understanding by Search Engines: Structured data serves as a conduit for facilitating a deeper understanding of a webpage's content by search engine algorithms. Through the strategic application of schema markup, website owners provide search engines with valuable context regarding the nature of their content. For instance, schema markup can delineate that a webpage pertains specifically to a book, thereby enabling search engines to extract and display relevant information such as the author's name, the book's title, and user reviews. This heightened understanding by search engines contributes to more accurate indexing and ranking of the website's content, ultimately bolstering its visibility and relevance within search results.

Voice Search Optimisation: In the era of voice search proliferation, structured data assumes heightened significance as an integral component of voice search optimisation strategies. Voice-enabled devices rely heavily on structured data to deliver concise and accurate responses to user queries. By incorporating schema markup into their web pages, website owners enhance the likelihood of their content being featured prominently in voice search results. This proactive approach to voice search optimisation positions websites to capitalise on the growing trend of voice-enabled search interfaces, thereby expanding their reach and relevance in the digital landscape.

Support for Emerging Technologies: Structured data serves as a foundational framework that underpins the functionality of emerging technologies and innovations in the digital sphere. For instance, Google's Knowledge Graph leverages structured data to furnish detailed insights into entities such as people, places, and objects. By embracing structured data, website owners future-proof their content, ensuring its compatibility and accessibility across evolving technological landscapes. This forward-thinking approach enables websites to remain at the forefront of technological advancements, maintaining their relevance and visibility amidst dynamic digital environments.

Types of Structured Data

Structured data encompasses a diverse array of markup types, each tailored to enhance the visibility, relevance, and user experience of specific content types on websites. While the examples provided below represent only a subset of the comprehensive range of structured data available, they offer a glimpse into the versatility and applicability of schema markup across various digital contexts. Here are some common examples.

Articles: Structured data markup for articles enables website owners to enrich the visibility of their journalistic or editorial content within search engine results. By annotating key elements such as headlines, featured images, publication dates, and author information, webmasters can provide search engines with invaluable context about the nature and relevance of their articles. This facilitates more accurate indexing and presentation of article listings in SERPs, ultimately increasing the likelihood of user engagement and click-through.

Products: E-commerce websites can leverage structured data markup for products to convey comprehensive information about their merchandise directly within search results. From prices and availability to customer reviews and ratings, product schema markup enables search engines to showcase rich snippets that offer users a detailed overview of the products on offer. This enhanced visibility and accessibility can significantly influence purchasing decisions, driving traffic and conversions for online retailers.

Events: Marking up event-related content with structured data allows website owners to effectively promote and disseminate information about upcoming events. By including details such as event dates, locations, ticket prices, and organiser information, event schema markup enables search engines to present relevant event listings in SERPs. This not only enhances the visibility of events but also facilitates user engagement and attendance through streamlined access to pertinent information.

Local Businesses: Local businesses can optimise their online presence and enhance local SEO performance through structured data markup. By providing essential business information such as address, phone number, business hours, and customer reviews, local business schema markup enables search engines to accurately represent and promote local establishments in geographic-specific search results. This heightened visibility within local search listings fosters increased foot traffic and customer engagement for brick-and-mortar businesses.

Recipes: Structured data markup for recipes empowers culinary websites to showcase their culinary creations with rich and informative snippets in search results. By annotating ingredients, cooking times, preparation methods, and nutritional information, recipe schema markup enhances the visibility and attractiveness of recipe listings in SERPs. This enables users to make informed decisions about recipe selection while driving traffic and engagement for food-related websites.

Breadcrumbs: Breadcrumbs structured data aids in improving website navigation and user experience by providing clear hierarchical pathways for users and search engines to navigate site content. By implementing breadcrumb navigation markup, website owners enable users to understand the hierarchical structure of their site and easily navigate between different levels of content. This not only enhances usability but also facilitates more efficient crawling and indexing by search engine bots, thereby optimising the overall discoverability of website content.

While the aforementioned examples represent just a fraction of the myriad structured data markup types available, they underscore the versatility and utility of schema markup in enhancing website visibility, user experience, and search engine performance across diverse digital contexts. Website owners are encouraged to explore and leverage the full spectrum of structured data markup options available, tailoring their implementation strategies to suit the unique content and objectives of their websites.

Implementing Schema Markup

Implementing schema markup is a crucial aspect of modern SEO strategies, facilitating enhanced visibility, richer search results, and improved user engagement. While manual implementation of schema markup is feasible for smaller websites with limited content, it can become arduous and error-prone for larger, more complex sites. Fortunately, there exists a plethora of tools and plugins designed to streamline and automate the process of adding structured data to websites, alleviating the burden on webmasters and ensuring consistent and accurate markup across all pages.

One such tool is Google's Structured Data Markup Helper, a user-friendly resource that empowers webmasters to mark up their web pages with schema markup using a simple point-and-click interface. This intuitive tool guides users through the process of identifying and annotating key elements on their web pages, generating structured data code snippets that can be seamlessly integrated into the HTML code. By leveraging the Structured Data Markup Helper, website owners can expedite the implementation of schema markup without requiring advanced technical expertise, thus saving time and minimising the risk of errors.

For WordPress users, the Yoast SEO plugin emerges as a valuable ally in the quest for optimised schema markup. Beyond its renowned SEO optimisation features, Yoast SEO offers built-in functionality for automatically adding structured data to WordPress websites. With just a few clicks, users can configure the plugin to generate and insert schema markup for various content types, including articles, products, events, and more. This automated approach streamlines the process of schema markup implementation, enabling WordPress users to enhance their search presence with minimal effort.

Furthermore, dedicated platforms like Schema App offer comprehensive solutions for adding structured data to websites of all sizes and complexities. These advanced tools provide sophisticated functionality for creating, managing, and deploying schema markup across diverse content types and platforms. From customisable templates and schema generation wizards to robust validation and testing tools, Schema App equips webmasters with the resources they need to implement structured data effectively and efficiently. Additionally, Schema App offers ongoing support and updates to ensure compliance with evolving schema standards and search engine algorithms.

By leveraging these tools and plugins, website owners can unlock the full potential of schema markup to elevate their SEO performance and drive tangible results. Whether through intuitive point-and-click interfaces, seamless WordPress integrations, or comprehensive schema management platforms, these solutions empower webmasters to harness the power of structured data without being encumbered by technical complexities. As the importance of schema markup continues to grow in the digital landscape, investing in these tools represents a strategic imperative for organisations seeking to maximise their online visibility and competitiveness.

Testing and Monitoring Structured Data

After implementing structured data, it's crucial to test it to ensure that it's correctly formatted and recognised by search engines. Google provides the **Rich Results Test** and the **Structured Data Testing Tool** to help you validate your markup. These tools will show you any errors or warnings in your structured data and how your rich snippets might appear in search results.

Monitoring the performance of your structured data is also essential. Google Search Console provides insights into how your structured data is performing, including the number of impressions and clicks your rich snippets are receiving. Regularly check Search Console for any issues or improvements related to your structured data.

Rich Snippets and Visual Search Enhancements

There are cutting-edge search result features that leverage structured data and schema markup to enrich search engine results and provide users with more visually appealing and informative experiences. These advanced functionalities go beyond traditional text-based search re- sults / listings, incorporating visual elements, interactive features, and contextual information to enhance the search experience and drive user engagement.

Rich snippets, generated through structured data markup, are en- hanced search listings that display additional information directly within search engine results pages (SERPs). These snippets can in- clude various elements such as images, star ratings, prices, availability, and other relevant data, providing users with valuable insights into the content of web pages before they even click on the search result. By presenting users with more comprehensive previews of web page content, rich snippets improve search result visibility, attract user at- tention, and increase the likelihood of clicks and conversions.

Visual search enhancements build upon the foundation of struc- tured data and schema markup to enable users to search for informa- tion using images rather than text. Visual search technology analyses the content of images, identifies objects, landmarks, products, and other visual elements, and retrieves relevant search results based on vi- sual similarity. This innovative approach to search empowers users to explore the web in a more intuitive and interactive manner, enabling them to discover new content, products, and information simply by uploading or snapping a photo.

The integration of rich snippets and visual search enhancements into search engine results represents a paradigm shift in how users in- teract with search engines and consume digital content. By leveraging structured data and schema markup to enhance the presentation and accessibility of search results, search engines are able to deliver more relevant, engaging, and personalised experiences to users across various devices and platforms.

Benefits of Rich Snippets:

Enhanced Visibility: Rich snippets make search results more visually appealing and attention-grabbing, increasing the likelihood of clicks and interactions.

Improved Click-Through Rates (CTR): By providing users with additional information upfront, rich snippets encourage higher CTRs and drive more traffic to web pages.

Increased User Engagement: Rich snippets offer users more context and insight into web page content, leading to higher levels of engagement and interaction.

Enhanced Brand Visibility: Rich snippets allow brands to showcase important information such as ratings, reviews, and pricing directly in search results, boosting brand visibility and credibility.

Competitive Advantage: Websites that implement rich snippets gain a competitive edge by standing out from competitors in search engine results and attracting more attention from users.

Benefits of Visual Search Enhancements:

Intuitive Search Experience: Visual search enables users to search for information using images, making the search process more intuitive and user-friendly.

Discoverability of Visual Content: Visual search helps users discover visual content, products, and information that may not be easily described in text-based searches.

Increased Engagement: Visual search enhances user engagement by providing more interactive and immersive search experiences that capture users' attention and interest.

Enhanced E-Commerce Experience: Visual search facilitates product discovery and comparison, allowing users to find and purchase products more easily and efficiently.

Accessibility for Visual Learners: Visual search caters to visual learners and individuals who prefer visual information over text-based content, making search more inclusive and accessible.

These are powerful tools that leverage structured data and schema markup to enhance search engine results and provide users with more engaging and interactive experiences. By implementing these advanced functionalities, websites can increase visibility, drive traffic, and improve user engagement, ultimately contributing to their overall success in the digital landscape.

The Buy-In Process

Acquiring internal buy-in for the allocation of a web developer's time towards implementing structured data and schema markup is a strategic endeavour that necessitates effective communication, alignment of objectives, and demonstration of tangible benefits. Convincing stakeholders of the value proposition associated with structured data requires a comprehensive approach that encompasses education, advocacy, and strategic planning. Below are several strategies to garner internal support for the integration of structured data and schema markup into a website:

Educate Stakeholders: Begin by educating key stakeholders, including executives, marketing teams, and IT personnel, about the importance and potential benefits of structured data and schema markup. Provide clear explanations of how these technologies function, their relevance to SEO strategies, and their impact on search engine visibility and user experience. Utilise case studies, industry reports, and real-world examples to illustrate the tangible advantages of structured data implementation.

Align with Organisational Goals: Position the integration of structured data and schema markup as a strategic initiative aligned with the organisation's broader objectives and priorities. Highlight how improved search engine visibility, enhanced user engagement, and increased website traffic contribute to overarching business goals such as brand awareness, lead generation, and revenue growth. Emphasise the long-term benefits and return on investment (ROI) associated with structured data implementation.

Showcase Competitive Insights: Conduct competitive analysis to identify industry peers or competitors who have successfully implemented structured data and schema markup. Highlight their achievements, such as improved search rankings, higher click-through rates (CTR), and enhanced user engagement, to demonstrate the competitive advantage gained through structured data adoption. Use this information to illustrate the potential risks of falling behind competitors who embrace advanced SEO techniques.

Provide Technical Guidance: Collaborate closely with IT and development teams to provide technical guidance and support for the implementation of structured data and schema markup. Offer training sessions, workshops, and documentation to familiarise developers with the syntax, best practices, and tools associated with structured data integration. Address any concerns or misconceptions regarding the complexity or resource requirements of implementing structured data, and emphasise the long-term benefits of investing in SEO enhancements.

Conduct Pilot Projects: Initiate small-scale pilot projects or proof-of-concept implementations to demonstrate the efficacy and feasibility of structured data integration. Select a subset of web pages or content types to serve as test cases for implementing schema markup, and measure key performance metrics such as search engine visibility, click-through rates, and user engagement. Present the results of pilot projects to stakeholders, showcasing the positive impact of structured data on website performance and SEO effectiveness.

Quantify Potential Benefits: Quantify the potential benefits of structured data implementation in terms of tangible outcomes such as increased organic traffic, higher search rankings, and improved conversion rates. Use data-driven analysis and projections to estimate the potential ROI of investing in structured data integration, taking into account factors such as anticipated traffic growth, user engagement metrics, and revenue generated from enhanced search visibility. Present these findings in a clear and compelling manner to justify the allocation of resources towards structured data initiatives.

Foster Cross-Functional Collaboration: Foster collaboration and alignment between marketing, IT, and other relevant departments to ensure cohesive execution of structured data initiatives. Encourage open communication, shared ownership, and mutual accountability for achieving SEO objectives and driving website performance improvements. Establish regular meetings, cross-functional working groups, and performance review sessions to monitor progress, address challenges, and optimise structured data implementation strategies.

By leveraging these strategies and effectively articulating the value proposition of structured data and schema markup, web developers can secure internal buy-in and support for implementing these advanced SEO techniques. By aligning structured data initiatives with organisational goals, providing technical guidance and support, and quantifying potential benefits, developers can position themselves as strategic partners in driving website success and achieving business objectives.

Latest Updates in Structured Data

In the ever-evolving landscape of SEO, staying updated with the latest developments in structured data is crucial for maintaining and enhancing a website's visibility and performance. The integration of structured data and schema markup has been significantly refined and expanded over recent years, reflecting changes in technology, search engine algorithms, and user behaviour. This section explores the most recent updates and trends in structured data, drawing insights from the latest Google Search Quality Evaluator Guidelines and other authoritative sources.

Evolution of Schema Markup

Schema.org, the primary repository of structured data vocabularies, continually updates and expands its collection to accommodate new types of content and emerging technologies. Recent additions and updates have focused on improving the representation of complex data types, such as datasets, financial transactions, and health-related information. These updates ensure that search engines can better understand and display these types of content, improving user experience and engagement.

Datasets and Structured Data: With the increasing importance of big data and open data initiatives, Schema.org has introduced and refined vocabularies for datasets. These improvements enable organisations to better structure their data for search engines, facilitating enhanced discoverability and usability of large datasets. For instance, government websites and academic institutions can now provide more detailed and accessible information about their datasets through structured data.

Financial Transactions: As e-commerce continues to grow, structured data for financial transactions has become more sophisticated. Recent updates allow for more precise markup of transaction details, including payment methods, transaction types, and service fees. This granular level of detail helps search engines accurately present financial information, enhancing transparency and user trust.

Health and Medical Information: Given the critical nature of health information, recent updates to schema vocabularies focus on improving the accuracy and reliability of medical content. New properties and types for medical conditions, treatments, and healthcare providers have been added to ensure that users receive accurate and trustworthy information. This is particularly important for Your Money or Your Life (YMYL) pages, which are held to higher standards of accuracy and reliability.

Integration with AI and Machine Learning

Search engines increasingly leverage AI and machine learning to interpret and utilise structured data more effectively. Google's use of BERT (Bidirectional Encoder Representations from Transformers) and other advanced algorithms highlights the importance of providing well-structured data that these models can easily parse and understand. This integration allows for more nuanced and contextually accurate search results, benefiting users and content providers alike.

AI-Driven Enhancements: Google and other search engines use AI to enhance the interpretation of structured data, improving the relevance and accuracy of search results. For example, Google's BERT model can better understand the context provided by structured data, allowing for more precise answers to user queries. This is especially beneficial for complex queries that require a deep understanding of the content's context and nuances.

Contextual Understanding: Machine learning models are adept at understanding the relationships between different pieces of structured data. This ability allows search engines to provide more comprehensive and contextually relevant search results. For instance, a search for "best cameras 2024" can yield results that not only list top cameras but also provide rich snippets with reviews, ratings, and price comparisons, thanks to well-implemented structured data.

Keeping up with the latest updates and trends in structured data is crucial for any SEO strategy. By understanding and implementing these advancements, you can ensure that your website remains visible, relevant, and competitive in the ever-changing digital landscape. For a comprehensive list of structured data types and vocabularies, visit Schema.org, where you can explore the full range of options available for enhancing your website's search performance.

CHAPTER 6
SEO AND ACCESSIBILITY

The intersection between SEO and accessibility has become increasingly significant. Both disciplines share a common goal: to create a user-friendly experience that enables all individuals to access and engage with web content. Accessibility is fundamentally about ensuring that everyone, including people with disabilities, can navigate and use a website. When done correctly, the improvements made for accessibility can also have a profound impact on SEO, leading to better search engine rankings, increased traffic, and a more inclusive web presence.

To fully appreciate how accessibility improvements can benefit SEO, it's important to understand that search engines function similarly to users with disabilities, especially those relying on screen readers or other assistive technologies. Search engines, like these users, depend on clear and well-structured content to understand the relevance and context of a webpage. By making a website accessible, you are effectively optimising it for search engines as well. This synergy between accessibility and SEO can lead to numerous advantages, ranging from enhanced user experience to better rankings in search engine results pages (SERPs).

Enhanced Website Structure and Navigation

One of the primary aspects of accessibility is the creation of a logical and user-friendly website structure. This involves ensuring that your website's navigation is intuitive, with clear headings, labels, and easy-to-use menus. When these elements are well-structured, not only do they help users with disabilities navigate the site more easily, but they also make it easier for search engines to crawl and index your site. Search engines rely on the organisation of your website to understand the relationship between different pages and the importance of each section. A well-structured website is more likely to be fully indexed, improving your visibility in search results.

For example, proper use of HTML heading tags (H1, H2, H3, etc.) is crucial for both accessibility and SEO. Headings help users with screen readers navigate through content more efficiently, and they also provide search engines with a clear outline of the content hierarchy on your page. When headings are used correctly, search engines can better understand the context and structure of your content, which can lead to improved rankings for relevant queries.

Improved User Experience and Engagement Metrics

Accessibility enhancements contribute significantly to a better overall user experience, which is a critical factor in SEO. Websites that are easier to navigate, read, and interact with tend to keep users engaged longer. This translates to lower bounce rates, higher dwell times, and more interactions on the site—metrics that search engines increasingly consider when ranking pages. Google, in particular, has been clear about the importance of user experience as part of its ranking algorithm. Features such as mobile-friendliness, page speed, and ease of navigation, all of which are integral to accessibility, are now key ranking factors.

For instance, ensuring that your website is keyboard navigable not only helps users with physical disabilities but also makes your site easier for everyone to use. Keyboard navigation allows users to interact with your site without needing a mouse, which can be crucial for individuals with mobility impairments. This improvement, while primarily aimed at accessibility, can also enhance the user experience for those on mobile devices or those who simply prefer keyboard shortcuts. As a result, these improvements can lead to better engagement metrics, which in turn can boost your SEO performance.

Better Content Optimisation

Content optimisation is a cornerstone of SEO, and accessibility improvements can greatly enhance this process. For example, providing alternative text (alt text) for images is a key accessibility requirement that also serves as an important SEO tactic. Alt text helps visually impaired users understand the content of images by describing them in text form. At the same time, alt text provides search engines with additional context about the images on your site, which can help your images rank in search engine image results.

Moreover, when you create accessible content, you often need to simplify and clarify the language used, making it easier for all users to understand. This not only benefits users with cognitive disabilities but also makes your content more digestible for a broader audience, including search engines. Clear, concise, and well-organised content is more likely to rank higher because it is easier for search engines to parse and index. Additionally, accessible content often requires the use of descriptive link text, which can enhance the relevance of your links in the eyes of search engines.

Increased Mobile Usability

As mobile usage continues to dominate web traffic, ensuring that your website is accessible on all devices has become a critical factor for both accessibility and SEO. Google's mobile-first indexing means that the mobile version of your website is now the primary version used for ranking and indexing. Therefore, improving mobile accessibility directly benefits your SEO efforts.

Accessibility features such as larger buttons, scalable fonts, and responsive design contribute to a better mobile experience for all users. These enhancements make it easier for users to interact with your website on smaller screens, reducing frustration and increasing the likelihood of engagement. For SEO, this means that your site is more likely to perform well in mobile search results, particularly in local searches where mobile devices are often used.

Compliance with Web Standards and SEO Best Practices

Implementing accessibility features often requires adherence to established web standards, such as the Web Content Accessibility Guidelines (WCAG). These standards align closely with many SEO best practices. For example, WCAG encourages the use of semantic HTML, which helps both assistive technologies and search engines understand the content and structure of a webpage. Semantic HTML tags, such as `<article>`, `<section>`, and `<nav>`, provide meaningful information about the content they enclose, improving both accessibility and SEO.

Additionally, accessibility improvements often involve optimising page load times, as slow-loading pages can be particularly problematic for users with disabilities. Faster load times not only improve accessibility but are also a well-known ranking factor for search engines. By optimising your website for speed, you are simultaneously enhancing its accessibility and improving its chances of ranking higher in search results.

Broader Audience Reach

By making your website accessible, you open it up to a broader audience, including people with disabilities who might otherwise be unable to access your content. This not only fulfils an ethical responsibility but also has practical SEO benefits. A more inclusive website can attract a larger number of visitors, which can lead to more traffic, more engagement, and ultimately better rankings. Search engines recognise when a site is catering to a diverse audience and often reward this inclusivity with better visibility.

Moreover, accessibility can lead to increased social sharing and backlinks, as users are more likely to share content that is easy to consume and navigate. Social signals and backlinks are important factors in SEO, and a site that is accessible and user-friendly is more likely to earn these valuable endorsements.

Reduced Risk of Penalties and Improved Compliance

Finally, improving accessibility can help you avoid potential legal issues and penalties associated with non-compliance. In many countries, including the United States, there are legal requirements for website accessibility, particularly for businesses and government entities. Failure to comply with these regulations can result in lawsuits, fines, and damage to your brand's reputation. While legal compliance is the primary motivation for many organisations to improve accessibility, the SEO benefits that come with it are a significant added bonus.

By ensuring your website is accessible, you reduce the risk of facing penalties from both legal bodies and search engines. Search engines are increasingly prioritising websites that provide a good user experience, and accessibility is a key component of this. Sites that fail to meet accessibility standards may be penalised by search engines, resulting in lower rankings and decreased visibility.

The relationship between SEO and accessibility is one of mutual benefit. Improvements made to enhance the accessibility of a website not only ensure that it is usable by all individuals, regardless of their abilities, but also contribute to better SEO performance. By focusing on accessibility, you are effectively optimising your site for search engines, improving user experience, and reaching a wider audience. In today's digital landscape, where inclusivity and user-centred design are paramount, the integration of accessibility and SEO is not just a best practice—it's a necessity.

Tools for Auditing and Improving Website Accessibility

In the modern digital landscape, ensuring that a website is accessible to all users, including those with disabilities, is not just a matter of ethical responsibility but also a crucial aspect of creating a user-friendly experience that can significantly benefit SEO. While the concept of accessibility may seem daunting, especially for those unfamiliar with the technical aspects, a wide range of tools is available to help website owners audit and improve their site's accessibility. These tools not only identify areas where a website may be lacking in accessibility but also provide actionable insights and recommendations for improvements.

Using the right tools can make the process of auditing and improving website accessibility much more manageable, ensuring that your site meets the necessary standards and offers an inclusive experience for all users. Moreover, these tools can help you align your site with SEO best practices, given the strong correlation between accessibility and search engine optimisation. Let's delve into some of the most effective tools for auditing and improving website accessibility and how they contribute to enhancing both the user experience and SEO performance.

Automated accessibility checkers are tools that scan your website and identify potential accessibility issues based on established guidelines such as the Web Content Accessibility Guidelines (WCAG). These tools are particularly useful for quickly identifying common issues that might otherwise go unnoticed. They provide a detailed report of any errors or warnings, along with suggestions for how to fix them.

One of the most popular automated checkers is **WAVE (Web Accessibility Evaluation Tool)**. Developed by WebAIM, WAVE provides a visual representation of your website's accessibility issues by overlaying icons and indicators directly onto your webpage. This makes it easy to see exactly where problems lie and understand how they impact the user experience. WAVE checks for a wide range of accessibility issues, including missing alt text, low contrast between text and background, and improper use of HTML elements.

Another powerful tool is **Axe by Deque Systems**, which is available as a browser extension and an API. Axe focuses on identifying accessibility issues with high accuracy, ensuring that you don't get overwhelmed by false positives. It integrates seamlessly with developer tools, allowing for real-time analysis of web pages and the ability to test dynamic content.

Google Lighthouse is another tool that deserves mention. While Lighthouse is primarily known for its performance auditing capabilities, it also includes a robust accessibility audit feature. By running a

Lighthouse report, you can quickly assess your website's accessibility and receive scores based on various criteria, along with specific recommendations for improvement. Because Lighthouse is integrated into Google Chrome's developer tools, it's easily accessible and can be run on any webpage with just a few clicks.

One of the most critical aspects of website accessibility is ensuring that your content can be effectively navigated and understood by users who rely on screen readers. Screen readers convert text and other visual elements on a webpage into synthesised speech or braille, allowing visually impaired users to interact with the site. Testing your website with a screen reader is essential to ensure that it delivers a positive experience for these users.

NVDA (NonVisual Desktop Access) is a free, open-source screen reader that is widely used by both developers and users with visual impairments. NVDA allows you to navigate your website as a visually impaired user would, providing valuable insights into how your content is presented and interacted with through a screen reader. By using NVDA, you can identify potential issues such as improperly labelled buttons, inaccessible forms, or confusing navigation structures that could hinder the user experience.

For Mac users, **VoiceOver** is the built-in screen reader that comes with macOS. VoiceOver provides a comprehensive testing environment and offers features such as rotor controls, which allow for quick navigation through headings, links, and form controls. Testing your website with VoiceOver can help ensure that it is accessible to users on Apple devices, which are commonly used by those with disabilities due to their strong focus on accessibility.

JAWS (Job Access With Speech) is another screen reader widely used by visually impaired users, particularly in professional and educational settings. JAWS is a paid software with advanced features, making it one of the most powerful tools for screen reader testing. Using JAWS to test your website can help you identify complex accessibility issues that might not be caught by other screen readers, providing a more thorough understanding of how accessible your site truly is.

Colour contrast plays a vital role in web accessibility, particularly for users with visual impairments such as colour blindness. Ensuring that text and other visual elements have sufficient contrast against their background is crucial for readability. Low contrast can make content difficult to read, leading to a poor user experience and potentially lower engagement.

The Contrast Checker by WebAIM is a simple yet effective tool for evaluating the contrast ratio of text and background colours on your website. By entering the hex codes for your foreground and background colours, the tool calculates the contrast ratio and compares it against the minimum thresholds set by WCAG. The tool provides instant feedback on whether your colour choices meet the required standards and suggests adjustments if they do not.

Color Oracle is another useful tool, particularly for testing how your website appears to users with colour blindness. Color Oracle simulates various types of colour blindness and allows you to see how your website looks through the eyes of someone with a colour vision deficiency. This perspective is invaluable for ensuring that all users, regardless of their ability to perceive colour, can interact with your content effectively.

Adobe's Color Contrast Analyser is another option that offers a more integrated approach for designers working within the Adobe ecosystem. This tool provides real-time contrast analysis within Adobe XD, Photoshop, and other design software, allowing you to address contrast issues during the design phase before they even make it to the live site.

For many users with physical disabilities, navigating a website using a mouse is not an option. Instead, they rely on keyboard navigation to move through web pages. Ensuring that your website is fully navigable by keyboard is a key component of accessibility, and several tools can help you test and improve keyboard accessibility.

Focus Visible is a Chrome extension that highlights the focusable elements on your webpage, such as links, buttons, and form fields. As you tab through your site, Focus Visible shows you where the keyboard focus is, allowing you to see if it moves logically from one element to the next. This tool helps identify areas where keyboard navigation might be hindered, such as unresponsive buttons or hidden elements that cannot be reached via keyboard.

Tablin is another tool that specifically tests for keyboard accessibility. It simulates keyboard navigation by highlighting the path a user would take when using the tab key to move through interactive elements on your website. Tablin helps you identify any elements that are not accessible by keyboard, such as non-interactive divs or improperly coded custom elements, and provides guidance on how to make these elements keyboard-friendly.

NoCoffee is a Chrome extension that provides a comprehensive suite of simulations to test for various visual impairments, including scenarios where users may have to rely solely on keyboard navigation. NoCoffee helps you understand how users with different accessibility needs interact with your site and offers insights into areas that may require improvement.

Forms are an integral part of many websites, allowing users to sign up, make purchases, contact support, and more. However, forms can often be a source of frustration for users with disabilities if they are not designed and coded with accessibility in mind. Several tools are available to audit and improve the accessibility of forms on your website.

Form Validator is a tool that checks for common accessibility issues in form design, such as missing labels, improperly associated form fields, and inaccessible error messages. By running your forms through this validator, you can ensure that they meet accessibility standards and are usable by all individuals, including those using screen readers or other assistive technologies.

Totally is a JavaScript-based tool that provides a visual overlay on your website, highlighting accessibility issues in real time. It includes a module specifically for forms, which checks for the presence of labels, the correct association of input fields, and the accessibility of error handling mechanisms. Totally's real-time feedback is particularly useful for developers who need to test and adjust forms on the fly.

The Inclusive Components Form Pattern is not a tool per se but a comprehensive guide to building accessible forms. Written by accessibility expert Heydon Pickering, this guide covers everything from basic form structure to advanced techniques for making complex forms accessible. By following the best practices outlined in this guide, you can ensure that your forms are not only functional but also inclusive for all users.

For those looking for an all-in-one solution, comprehensive accessibility suites offer a range of tools and features designed to audit and improve various aspects of web accessibility. These suites are ideal for larger organisations or websites with complex accessibility needs.

Siteimprove Accessibility is a leading platform that provides a full suite of tools for auditing and improving web accessibility. It offers automated scans for accessibility issues, detailed reports, and suggestions for remediation. Siteimprove also includes tools for monitoring ongoing compliance with accessibility standards, ensuring that your website remains accessible over time. The platform integrates with popular CMSs and offers collaboration features, making it easy for teams to work together on accessibility improvements.

Monsido is another comprehensive accessibility platform that provides automated accessibility testing, reporting, and monitoring. Monsido's user-friendly interface and in-depth analytics make it easy to identify accessibility issues and track progress over time. The platform also includes tools for optimising content for SEO, highlighting the strong relationship between accessibility and search engine performance.

Deque's WorldSpace Comply is an enterprise-level solution that offers robust accessibility testing and monitoring capabilities. WorldSpace Comply integrates with development workflows, allowing teams to catch and fix accessibility issues during the design and development phases. The platform also provides detailed reports and dashboards, helping organisations maintain compliance with accessibility standards across large, complex websites.

Implementing Accessibility Enhancements

While tools can provide invaluable assistance in identifying and addressing accessibility issues, the real challenge lies in the implementation of the recommended changes. Accessibility enhancements require a systematic approach that involves developers, designers, content creators, and other stakeholders working together to create an inclusive online environment. The following strategies can help ensure that accessibility improvements are effectively integrated into your website, benefiting both users and SEO.

One of the most effective ways to enhance website accessibility is to integrate accessibility considerations into the design process from the very beginning. This proactive approach ensures that accessibility is not an afterthought but a fundamental aspect of the website's architecture and user experience. Designers should be well-versed in accessibility principles, such as ensuring sufficient colour contrast, designing for keyboard navigation, and creating intuitive layouts that are easy to navigate.

Design Systems and Pattern Libraries: Developing a design system or pattern library that includes accessibility guidelines can be a powerful tool in maintaining consistency across your website. These resources provide reusable components and templates that adhere to accessibility standards, making it easier for designers and developers to create accessible web pages. By incorporating accessible design patterns from the start, you reduce the likelihood of needing extensive revisions later in the development process.

Improving website accessibility requires collaboration between various teams, including design, development, content creation, and quality assurance. Regular communication and collaboration ensure that everyone involved understands the importance of accessibility and is working towards the same goals.

Cross-Disciplinary Training: Providing cross-disciplinary training on accessibility can help bridge the gap between different teams. For example, developers might need to understand the design principles that impact accessibility, while content creators might need to learn how to write alt text or structure content for screen readers. By fostering a culture of shared knowledge and responsibility, you can create a more cohesive and effective approach to accessibility.

Website accessibility is not a one-time project but an ongoing commitment. As your website evolves, new content is added, and updates are made, it's essential to continuously monitor and maintain accessibility standards. Regular audits and user testing should be part of your ongoing maintenance strategy to ensure that your site remains accessible to all users.

Automated Testing Integration: Integrating automated accessibility testing into your development pipeline can help catch issues early. Tools like **Axe Core** can be integrated into continuous integration/continuous deployment (CI/CD) workflows, automatically running accessibility tests whenever code is pushed to the repository. This ensures that accessibility remains a priority throughout the development lifecycle and that new issues are addressed before they reach production.

User Feedback and Testing: In addition to automated testing, gathering feedback from users with disabilities is crucial. Conducting usability testing sessions with users who rely on assistive technologies can provide valuable insights into real-world accessibility challenges. This feedback can guide further improvements and ensure that your website truly meets the needs of all users.

Transparency about your website's accessibility efforts is important for building trust with users and demonstrating your commitment to inclusivity. Publishing an accessibility statement on your website can inform users about the steps you've taken to make your site accessible and provide information on how they can report any issues they encounter.

Creating an Accessibility Statement: An accessibility statement should outline your commitment to accessibility, describe the standards you've used (such as WCAG), and provide contact information for users to report accessibility barriers. It's also helpful to include information about the tools and processes you've used to audit and improve accessibility, as well as any ongoing efforts to maintain compliance.

Internal Documentation: Documenting your accessibility practices internally is also important. This documentation should include guidelines for designing, developing, and maintaining accessible content, as well as records of past audits, issues identified, and steps taken to address them. Keeping thorough documentation ensures that accessibility knowledge is retained within your organisation and can be passed on as team members change.

Finally, it's important to recognise the SEO benefits that can result from improving website accessibility. Many accessibility enhancements align closely with SEO best practices, leading to a more search-friendly website overall.

Enhanced User Experience: Accessibility improvements often lead to a better user experience for all visitors, not just those with disabilities. A well-structured, easy-to-navigate website is likely to keep users engaged longer, reduce bounce rates, and increase the likelihood of return visits—all of which are positive signals to search engines.

Improved Content Visibility: Proper use of alt text, headings, and semantic HTML not only makes your content more accessible to screen readers but also helps search engines better understand and index your content. This can lead to improved visibility in search results, particularly for image searches and rich snippets.

Reduced Legal Risks: Ensuring your website is accessible can also help mitigate the risk of legal action related to non-compliance with accessibility laws and regulations. While this is not directly related to SEO, avoiding legal issues helps maintain your site's reputation and prevents disruptions that could negatively impact your online presence.

Implementing tools for auditing and improving website accessibility is a critical step in creating an inclusive digital environment that benefits all users. By using automated checkers, screen reader testing, colour contrast analysers, and comprehensive accessibility suites, you can identify and address accessibility issues effectively. Moreover, integrating accessibility into your design process, fostering collaboration between teams, and maintaining continuous monitoring are key strategies to ensure your website remains accessible over time.

Not only do these efforts enhance the user experience, but they also contribute to better SEO performance by improving content visibility, user engagement, and compliance with search engine guidelines. By prioritising accessibility, you create a website that is welcoming to all users and well-positioned to succeed in the competitive online landscape.

CHAPTER 7
SEO "AUDITS"

The concept of SEO "audits" often surfaces as a purported silver bullet for enhancing a website's search engine performance. Traditionally, an SEO audit is presented as a comprehensive review of a website's technical health and link profile. However, in today's landscape, the notion of a one-time SEO audit is not only outdated but potentially misleading. An SEO audit, in its conventional sense, is akin to a dusty document relegated to a shelf, losing relevance as search engines continuously evolve and user behaviour shifts.

The idea of an SEO audit is rooted in the past, a time when the digital ecosystem was less complex and search engine algorithms were more predictable. Back then, a detailed document outlining the current state of a website's SEO, complete with recommendations, might have sufficed. But the pace at which digital marketing and SEO evolve today renders such static reports obsolete almost as soon as they are completed.

Imagine conducting an SEO audit like performing a health checkup on a car before a long road trip. You meticulously inspect the engine, check the tire pressure, and ensure all fluids are at optimal levels. Once everything looks good, you embark on your journey, confident that your car is in peak condition. However, just a few miles down the road, the conditions change - potholes, inclement weather, and varying terrain all demand constant attention and adjustments. A one-time inspection, no matter how thorough, cannot account for these real-time variables. Similarly, an SEO audit provides a snapshot of your website's health at a specific moment in time but fails to account for the continuous changes in search algorithms, competitor strategies, and user behaviour that impact your site's performance.

The Pitfalls of Traditional SEO Audits

The allure of an SEO audit lies in its promise of a comprehensive, one-time fix for all your website's SEO issues. Scammers and unscrupulous practitioners exploit this promise, offering so-called "complete" SEO audits for a few hundred euro. These audits often result in lengthy reports filled with technical jargon and generic recommendations, which, at best, provide a temporary improvement and, at worst, lead you astray. Investing in these static audits is akin to throwing money into the wind—€500 for a report that will soon be outdated, gathering dust as your competitors move ahead with agile, adaptive strategies. And to make matters worse, they were just created using some tools. Tools cannot do SEO, people use tools to do SEO faster.

The Organic Search Strategy

Instead of relying on outdated audits, what you truly need is a dynamic, ongoing organic search strategy. This strategy includes an initial assessment, much like an audit, but extends far beyond that to encompass continuous monitoring, updating, and optimisation. It is a holistic approach that integrates technical SEO, content, link building, and performance analysis into a cohesive, adaptable framework.

Initial Website Technical Assessment: The starting point of any effective SEO strategy is a thorough technical assessment of your website. This involves identifying and rectifying issues related to site speed, mobile-friendliness, crawlability, and indexability. However, unlike a traditional audit, this technical assessment is the beginning, not the end. It sets the foundation for ongoing optimisation.

Review of Link Profile: Understanding and improving your link profile is crucial. This involves analysing your current backlinks, identifying toxic links, and developing a strategy for acquiring high-quality backlinks. But the process does not stop here. Link building is an ongoing effort that requires continuous attention and strategic outreach.

Benchmarking Visibility: Establishing benchmarks for your website's visibility in search engine results is essential for measuring progress. However, these benchmarks should be revisited regularly. Continuous tracking and analysis of your rankings, organic traffic, and user engagement metrics will provide insights into the effectiveness of your SEO efforts and highlight areas for improvement.

Content Strategy and Optimisation: Content is at the heart of any effective SEO strategy. An initial content audit can help identify gaps and opportunities, but content optimisation is an ongoing process. Regularly updating existing content, creating new, high-quality content, and aligning your content strategy with evolving user intent and search trends are crucial for maintaining and improving your search visibility.

Performance Monitoring and Adaptation: The digital landscape is constantly changing, and your SEO strategy must adapt accordingly. Implementing tools for real-time performance monitoring, such as Google Analytics and Search Console, enables you to track key metrics, identify issues promptly, and make data-driven adjustments. Regular performance reviews and strategic adjustments ensure that your SEO efforts remain aligned with your business goals and market dynamics.

Tools for Auditing

In the dynamic world of SEO, leveraging the right tools can make all the difference between a lacklustre performance and a robust, high-ranking website. A comprehensive SEO audit requires a suite of tools designed to analyse various aspects of your website, from technical health to content quality and backlink profile. This section delves into some of the most effective tools available for conducting thorough SEO audits, ensuring you have the resources needed to optimise every facet of your online presence.

Google Search Console is an indispensable tool for any SEO audit. It provides a wealth of information directly from Google, making it an authoritative source for understanding how your site is performing in search results. The key features include Search Analytics, which offers insights into how your site appears in search results, including clicks, impressions, click-through rates, and average position. The Coverage Report identifies pages that are indexed and those that have encountered errors, helping you address issues that might prevent your content from being found. Sitemaps allow you to submit your sitemaps to Google, ensuring that all your pages are crawled and indexed efficiently. Mobile Usability highlights mobile usability issues, helping you ensure your site provides a good experience for mobile users.

Google Analytics complements Search Console by offering deeper insights into user behaviour on your website. The Audience Overview provides demographic information about your visitors, including age, gender, and location. Behaviour Flow visualises the paths users take through your site, helping you understand how they interact with your content. Conversion Tracking allows you to set up goals and track conversions, giving you insight into how effectively your site drives desired actions.

Screaming Frog SEO Spider is a powerful desktop application that crawls websites and provides detailed information about technical SEO issues. It performs a comprehensive crawl of your entire website to identify issues such as broken links, duplicate content, and redirect chains. The tool also provides on-page SEO analysis, offering insights into elements like titles, meta descriptions, headers, and images. Additionally, it can create XML sitemaps to ensure search engines can effectively crawl and index your site.

Ahrefs is a versatile tool known for its robust backlink analysis capabilities, but it also offers comprehensive features for conducting SEO audits. The Site Explorer analyses your backlink profile, providing insights into referring domains, anchor text distribution, and lost or broken links. The Content Explorer helps identify high-performing content in your niche, offering ideas for content creation and optimisation. Ahrefs' Site Audit performs a thorough audit of your website, identifying issues related to performance, HTML tags, social tags, content quality, and more.

SEMrush is an all-in-one SEO tool that offers a wide range of features for auditing and optimising your website. The Site Audit feature conducts a detailed audit of your website, identifying issues related to crawlability, HTTPS implementation, site performance, and more. Keyword Research provides comprehensive keyword analysis, including search volume, keyword difficulty, and competitive analysis. Position Tracking monitors your rankings for targeted keywords over time, allowing you to track your SEO progress and adjust your strategy as needed.

Moz Pro is another comprehensive SEO tool that offers a variety of features for conducting audits and improving your site's performance. The Site Crawl feature identifies and fixes technical SEO issues, such as broken links, duplicate content, and missing tags. Keyword Explorer offers insights into keyword opportunities, helping you target the most relevant and valuable search terms. Link Explorer analyses your backlink profile, providing metrics such as Domain Authority (DA) and Page Authority (PA) to help you assess the quality of your backlinks.

GTmetrix is a specialised tool focused on analysing and improving site speed and performance. It provides detailed reports on page load times, total page size, and the number of requests, along with actionable recommendations for improvement. The Video Playback feature allows you to see a video of your page loading, helping you identify and understand performance bottlenecks. Historical Data tracks your performance over time, allowing you to see the impact of your optimisation efforts.

DeepCrawl is a cloud-based tool designed for large-scale website audits. It performs extensive crawls of large websites, identifying issues such as broken links, duplicate content, and security vulnerabilities. Custom Reports allow you to create tailored reports specific to your needs, providing insights into areas like content quality, site structure, and more. API Integration allows DeepCrawl to integrate with other tools and platforms, such as Google Analytics and Search Console, to provide a unified view of your SEO data.

Ubersuggest, developed by Neil Patel, is a user-friendly SEO tool that provides a range of features for keyword research, site audits, and competitive analysis. The Keyword Analysis feature offers insights into keyword search volume, competition, and trends. The Site Audit feature provides an overview of your site's health, including issues related to SEO, speed, and usability. The Content Ideas feature generates content ideas based on what's performing well in your niche, helping you create engaging and relevant content.

For WordPress users, Yoast SEO is a well-known plugin that has long been a staple for many looking to optimise their on-page SEO. However, it's important to note that Yoast's approach has become somewhat outdated. The tool tends to focus heavily on keyword usage rather than engaging, topic-led content. This approach can lead to content that is optimised for search engines but may not resonate well with users. While Yoast SEO still offers valuable features such as XML sitemaps and basic SEO analysis, relying solely on its recommendations can result in missed opportunities for creating truly engaging and high-quality content.

Combining Tools for a Holistic Audit

While each tool offers unique features and insights, the most effective SEO audits often involve a combination of these tools. By leveraging multiple tools, you can gain a comprehensive understanding of your site's strengths and weaknesses, ensuring no aspect of your SEO strategy is overlooked.

For example, you might use Google Search Console and Google Analytics to understand user behaviour and site performance, Screaming Frog and DeepCrawl for in-depth technical analysis, and Ahrefs or Moz for backlink analysis and keyword research. Combining the insights from these tools allows you to develop a holistic SEO strategy that addresses all aspects of your site's performance.

Conducting a thorough SEO audit requires a robust suite of tools that provide comprehensive insights into every aspect of your website. From technical SEO to content quality and backlink analysis, these tools enable you to identify issues, implement improvements, and monitor progress over time. By investing in the right tools and combining their strengths, you can ensure your SEO strategy is well-informed, effective, and capable of driving sustained organic growth. Avoid the pitfalls of superficial audits and embrace a comprehensive approach that leverages the full power of modern SEO tools.

CHAPTER 8
CONTENT STRATEGY: BEYOND "CONTENT MARKETING"

The term "content marketing" has become somewhat antiquated, often misinterpreted as simply creating and distributing content to attract customers. So, throwing shit at the wall. However, in today's landscape, a more holistic approach is required - one that goes beyond mere marketing. This is why I prefer the term "Content Strategy."

Content Strategy encompasses not just the creation and distribution of content, but also the careful planning, development, management, and governance of content. It's about being intentional with your content and ensuring that every piece serves a strategic purpose, aligns with your business goals, and adds genuine value to your audience.

A robust content strategy involves understanding your audience deeply, defining your brand's voice, and consistently delivering messages that resonate and engage. It requires a comprehensive understanding of your market, your competition, and, most importantly, your unique value proposition. This strategic approach ensures that your content is not just noise but a meaningful conversation with your audience that builds trust, fosters loyalty, and drives sustainable growth.

As a former journalist, I have many thoughts on content strategy.

If it doesn't add value, don't publish it; if it's not authentic, don't say it. Every piece of content should serve a clear purpose. Whether it's to inform, entertain, or inspire, it must add value to your audience's experience. Authenticity is non-negotiable; your content must reflect your brand's true voice and values.

The best response to a competitor's content is to innovate, not imitate. Instead of copying what others are doing, focus on what makes your brand unique. Innovation is key to standing out in a crowded market.

If you fear failure, you will likely never create anything worthy of going viral. Taking risks is essential for creativity. Not every piece of content will be a hit, but without taking chances, you'll never create anything truly remarkable.

You have power over your content strategy—not the market. Realise this, and you might find success. While you can't control market conditions, you can control your content. Focus on what you can influence and leverage that to your advantage.

First, define the message you want to convey; then create the content to reflect it. Clarity in messaging is crucial. Before creating content, be clear about what you want to say and ensure every piece aligns with that message.

No brand is authentic if it is not master of its content. Control over your content means having a clear, consistent voice and message that reflects your brand's identity.

Create content that lets your audience see themselves in your narrative. When your audience can relate to your content, they are more likely to engage with it. Make your content relatable and relevant to their experiences and aspirations.

Your brand becomes shaped by the quality of its content. High-quality content builds a strong, positive perception of your brand. It reflects your brand's commitment to providing value and excellence.

Eliminate your distractions; focus solely on creating valuable content. Distractions dilute the quality of your work. Stay focused on creating content that truly matters to your audience.

Don't over-explain your brand values. Show them through your content. Actions speak louder than words. Demonstrate your brand values through the stories you tell and the actions you take, rather than just talking about them.

Consistent content builds trust that quick fixes cannot. Trust is built over time through consistent, reliable content. Quick, one-off attempts rarely achieve lasting impact.

Sometimes even publishing is an act of bravery. Just go for it and be open to feedback, good or bad. Taking the step to publish can be daunting, but it's necessary. Be open to feedback and use it to improve.

No brand is more stagnant than one that never experiments with content. Stagnation is the enemy of growth. Experimenting with different types of content can lead to new insights and opportunities.

The most influential brands have control over their own narrative. Controlling your narrative means being proactive about what you share and how you share it. It's about being a leader in your space, not just a participant.

Don't be afraid of controversy. Embrace it. Controversy can drive engagement and discussion. As long as it aligns with your brand values, don't shy away from it.

Publish unpopular opinions. They make you more human. Unpopular opinions can spark conversation and show that your brand has a unique perspective. It humanises your brand and sets you apart.

Those who do not understand their audience cannot create compelling content. Knowing your audience is the foundation of effective content strategy. Without this understanding, your content will miss the mark.

Above all, there is one question to ask yourself: Why are you not demanding the best content for your audience? Your audience deserves the best. Demand excellence in every piece of content you produce.

Moving from Content Marketing to Content Strategy involves a shift from focusing on creating content to attract customers to taking a more holistic approach that views content as a strategic asset. Content marketing often emphasises quantity over quality and short-term gains over long-term value. In contrast, content strategy prioritises a deep understanding of the audience's needs, preferences, and behaviours, ensuring that every piece of content serves a strategic purpose and contributes to overarching business goals.

One of the key differences between content marketing and content strategy is the emphasis on audience understanding and engagement. Content marketing might focus on pushing out content based on keyword research and trends, but content strategy prioritises a deep understanding of the audience's needs, preferences, and behaviours. This means conducting thorough research to uncover insights about your audience and using these insights to inform your content creation and distribution.

Another critical aspect of content strategy is the focus on storytelling. Rather than just creating content for the sake of it, a strategic approach involves crafting narratives that resonate with your audience on an emotional level. Stories have the power to connect, inspire, and motivate, making your content more memorable and impactful.

Content Strategy also emphasises the importance of consistency and coherence. Your content should not only be high-quality but also consistent in tone, style, and messaging across all channels. This builds trust and recognition, making it easier for your audience to connect with your brand.

Furthermore, content strategy is about continuous improvement. It involves regularly reviewing and analysing the performance of your content to understand what works and what doesn't. This iterative process allows you to refine your strategy over time, ensuring that your content remains relevant and effective.

Moving from content marketing to content strategy involves a shift from quantity to quality, from short-term tactics to long-term planning, and from generic content to personalised, engaging narratives.

It requires a deep understanding of your audience, a commitment to excellence, and a willingness to experiment and adapt. By embracing content strategy, you can build a stronger, more meaningful connection with your audience and drive sustainable growth for your brand.

Creating a content strategy and calendar that balances user engagement and SEO effectiveness is both an art and a science. A well-crafted content strategy ensures that your content not only attracts and retains an audience but also ranks well in search engines, driving consistent organic traffic. This chapter delves into the intricacies of developing such a strategy, highlighting key considerations and best practices to ensure your content meets the dual goals of user satisfaction and SEO performance.

To begin with, it's essential to understand your audience deeply. Knowing who your target audience is, what their interests are, and how they search for information is the cornerstone of any successful content strategy. Conducting thorough audience research through surveys, interviews, and analysing web analytics can provide valuable insights into the needs and preferences of your audience. This research should inform every aspect of your content creation process, from topic selection to tone of voice and content format.

Once you have a clear understanding of your audience, the next step is to identify the key topics that will form the backbone of your content strategy. These topics should align with both your business objectives and the interests of your audience. Keyword research plays a crucial role here, helping you uncover the terms and phrases your audience uses when searching for information related to your industry. Tools like Google Keyword Planner, SEMrush, and Ahrefs can help you identify high-volume, low-competition keywords that can drive targeted traffic to your site.

However, a keyword-centric approach alone is not enough. Google's algorithms have evolved to prioritise content that demonstrates expertise, authoritativeness, and trustworthiness (E-E-A-T). This means your content needs to provide real value, backed by thorough research and credible sources. Creating in-depth, well-researched articles, guides, and resources that answer your audience's questions comprehensively can help establish your site as a trusted authority in your niche. Additionally, incorporating insights from subject matter experts and citing reputable sources can enhance the credibility and trustworthiness of your content.

A content calendar is an indispensable tool in executing your content strategy effectively. It provides a structured timeline for content creation and publication, ensuring that you consistently deliver fresh, relevant content to your audience. Start by mapping out a high-level overview of the topics you want to cover over a specified period, such as a quarter or a year. Then, break down these topics into individual pieces of content, assigning specific publication dates to each.

When creating your content calendar, it's important to balance evergreen content with timely, topical content. Evergreen content, which remains relevant and valuable over time, can drive sustained traffic and engagement. Examples include how-to guides, industry best practices, and comprehensive resource lists. On the other hand, topical content, which addresses current trends, news, or events, can drive spikes in traffic and engagement by capitalising on what's currently popular or relevant. By mixing evergreen and topical content, you can maintain a steady flow of traffic while also capturing bursts of interest.

In addition to topic selection and scheduling, a content calendar should also include detailed information about the production process. This includes assigning responsibilities to team members, setting deadlines for drafts and revisions, and planning for any necessary multimedia elements, such as images, videos, or infographics. Clear communication and collaboration among team members are crucial to ensuring that content is produced on time and to a high standard.

SEO considerations should be integrated into every stage of the content creation process. This starts with optimising your content for target keywords. However, avoid keyword stuffing, which can harm readability and user experience. Instead, focus on naturally incorporating keywords into your content, including in the title, headings, and throughout the body text. Additionally, make use of related keywords and semantic variations to help search engines understand the context and relevance of your content.

Meta tags, such as the title tag and meta description, are also important for SEO. Craft compelling, keyword-rich meta tags that accurately describe the content and encourage users to click through to your site. While meta descriptions do not directly impact rankings, they can influence click-through rates, which can indirectly affect your SEO performance.

Internal linking is another critical aspect of SEO that should be woven into your content strategy. Internal links help search engines understand the structure of your site and the relationship between different pages. They also help distribute link equity throughout your site, boosting the visibility of your most important pages. When creating content, look for opportunities to link to other relevant articles, guides, or resources on your site. This not only aids SEO but also enhances the user experience by providing additional valuable information.

Incorporating multimedia elements into your content can also enhance both user engagement and SEO performance. Videos, images, infographics, and interactive elements can make your content more engaging and easier to understand. These elements can also increase the time users spend on your site, reduce bounce rates, and encourage social sharing, all of which are positive signals to search engines. When using multimedia, ensure that they are optimised for SEO by including descriptive alt text for images, transcripts for videos, and appropriate metadata for all multimedia elements.

Promoting your content is just as important as creating it. Even the best content can go unnoticed without effective promotion. Utilise various channels to distribute your content, including social media, email marketing, and outreach to industry influencers and websites. Social media platforms can help amplify your content's reach and drive traffic back to your site. Tailor your promotion strategy to each platform's unique audience and features. For example, visual content may perform well on Instagram and Pinterest, while in-depth articles may be better suited for LinkedIn and Twitter.

Email marketing is another powerful tool for content promotion. Build and segment your email list to send targeted content to different audience segments. Personalised email campaigns can drive higher engagement and click-through rates. Consider using email automation to send content to subscribers at optimal times and track their engagement to refine your strategy.

Outreach to industry influencers and websites can also boost your content's visibility. Build relationships with influencers and websites in your niche and pitch your content for guest posts, mentions, or backlinks. High-quality backlinks from reputable sites can improve your site's authority and search rankings. Additionally, collaborating with influencers can expose your content to a broader audience and build credibility.

Monitoring and analysing the performance of your content is essential for refining your strategy. Use analytics tools to track key metrics, such as traffic, engagement, conversion rates, and SEO performance. Identify which pieces of content are performing well and which are not meeting expectations. Use these insights to adjust your content calendar, optimise underperforming content, and replicate the success of high-performing content.

User feedback is another valuable source of insights. Encourage readers to leave comments, ask questions, and provide feedback on your content. This feedback can highlight areas for improvement and inspire new content ideas. Additionally, engaging with your audience in the comments section or on social media can build a loyal community and enhance your brand's reputation.

Creating a content strategy and calendar that balances user engagement and SEO effectiveness requires careful planning, execution, and continuous optimisation. By understanding your audience, conducting thorough keyword research, and integrating SEO best practices into your content creation process, you can create content that resonates with users and performs well in search engines. A well-structured content calendar ensures consistent delivery of valuable content, while effective promotion and performance analysis help you refine your strategy and achieve long-term success. Embrace the dynamic nature of content marketing and SEO, and stay committed to delivering high-quality, relevant content that meets the needs of your audience.

CHAPTER 9

KEYWORD RESEARCH: STILL A CORNERSTONE OF SEO

The significance of keyword research cannot be overstated. While Google increasingly emphasises the creation of content that is topic-driven and user-centric, keywords continue to play a crucial role, especially in capturing intent-based searches for your actual products or services. Keyword research is not just about identifying words and phrases to sprinkle throughout your content; it's about deeply understanding how your audience searches for information, products, or services, and leveraging that insight to create content that meets their needs and expectations.

The Role of Keywords in Modern SEO

Keywords are the bridge between what people are searching for and the content you are providing to fill that need. They serve as a direct signal to search engines about the relevance of your content. However, the approach to using keywords has evolved dramatically over the years. Gone are the days when "keyword stuffing"—the practice of cramming as many keywords as possible into your content—was a viable strategy. Today, effective keyword usage is about context, relevance, and user intent.

While Google's algorithms have become sophisticated enough to understand and rank content based on topics and subtopics, keywords still hold a place of importance. They are particularly crucial when it comes to pure intent-based searches where users are looking for specific products or services. For example, if someone searches for "best running shoes for flat feet," they are likely ready to make a purchase or at least highly interested in detailed product information. By understanding and incorporating such intent-based keywords into your content, you can directly address the needs of potential customers at various stages of their buyer journey.

Understanding Your Audience Through Keyword Research

One of the fundamental benefits of keyword research is that it provides valuable insights into how your audience searches for what you do. This understanding goes beyond mere words; it encompasses the problems your audience faces, the solutions they seek, and the language they use. By analysing keyword data, you can identify common questions, concerns, and interests among your target demographic.

For instance, a thorough keyword analysis might reveal that your audience frequently searches for "how to reduce energy bills in winter." This insight not only informs you about a common pain point but also guides you in creating content that directly addresses this issue, such as an article titled "10 Tips to Reduce Your Energy Bills This Winter." Such content is likely to attract organic traffic, engage readers, and establish your authority on the subject.

Moreover, keyword research can help you uncover new opportunities for content creation. It allows you to identify gaps in the information available online and position yourself as a go-to resource for your audience. By consistently providing high-value content that aligns with your audience's search behaviour, you build trust and loyalty, which are critical for long-term success.

The Evolution of Keyword Usage

The practice of keyword stuffing, where content creators would excessively use target keywords in an attempt to manipulate search rankings, is now not only ineffective but also penalised by search engines. Today, search engine algorithms are adept at understanding context and intent, making it possible to rank well even without explicitly mentioning a target keyword multiple times.

In fact, Google's algorithms are sophisticated enough to understand and rank content based on the overall topic and the relationships between various pieces of information. This means that you can rank for certain queries without even mentioning the exact keyword on your page. For example, if your content thoroughly covers the topic of "reducing energy bills in winter" with comprehensive tips and advice, Google can rank your page for related searches like "winter energy saving tips" or "how to lower heating costs," even if these specific phrases are not used verbatim in your content.

This shift underscores the importance of creating high-quality, relevant content that addresses the needs and interests of your audience rather than focusing solely on keyword density. Search engines now prioritise user experience, meaning that factors such as page load speed, mobile-friendliness, and content structure are just as important, if not more so, than keyword placement.

Leveraging Keywords for Content Strategy

Despite the evolution in how keywords are used, they remain a cornerstone of any effective SEO strategy. Conducting comprehensive keyword research involves identifying primary keywords related to your business as well as long-tail keywords that capture specific queries and intent. This process helps you build a content strategy that is both comprehensive and targeted.

By mapping out a keyword strategy, you can create a roadmap for your content development efforts. This strategy ensures that your content is aligned with the needs and interests of your audience, making it more likely to attract organic traffic and achieve higher engagement rates. It also helps you stay focused on your business goals, ensuring that every piece of content you produce serves a strategic purpose.

While the landscape of SEO continues to evolve, the importance of keyword research remains steadfast. It is a powerful tool that provides deep insights into your audience's behaviour and needs, guiding you in creating content that is relevant, valuable, and engaging. By moving beyond outdated practices like keyword stuffing and embracing a more holistic, user-centric approach, you can leverage keywords to drive sustainable growth and success in your digital marketing efforts.

Techniques for Keyword Identification and Analysis

Keyword identification and analysis are fundamental components of an effective SEO strategy. They involve not only pinpointing the exact words and phrases your audience uses to search for information but also understanding the intent behind these searches and how best to address them. Here, we delve into the various techniques and tools that can help you identify and analyse keywords comprehensively.

Before diving into specific techniques, it's crucial to grasp the concept of search intent. Search intent refers to the reason behind a user's query—what they hope to accomplish by performing a search. Search intent can generally be classified into four categories: informational intent, navigational intent, transactional intent, and commercial investigation intent. Understanding the intent behind keywords helps you tailor your content to meet the specific needs of your audience, thereby improving relevance and engagement.

The first step in keyword identification is brainstorming potential keywords and phrases relevant to your business. Start with broad terms that describe your products or services. Think about the questions your customers frequently ask and the problems they face that your business can solve. Next, perform initial research using tools like Google Search Console, which provides insights into the keywords that are already driving traffic to your site. This data can serve as a foundation for further exploration.

There are several powerful tools available for conducting in-depth keyword research. These tools can help you uncover new keyword opportunities, analyse search volume and competition, and understand the competitive landscape.

Google Keyword Planner, originally designed for Google Ads, is invaluable for SEO as well. It helps you find keywords related to your business and provides data on search volume, competition, and keyword trends.

Ahrefs offers a comprehensive suite of SEO tools, including a robust keyword explorer. It provides detailed insights into keyword difficulty, search volume, and potential traffic, along with competitor analysis.

SEMrush is another all-in-one SEO tool that excels in keyword research. It offers keyword suggestions, search volume data, keyword difficulty scores, and competitor keyword analysis.

Moz Keyword Explorer provides an intuitive keyword research tool that offers keyword suggestions, search volume estimates, and SERP (Search Engine Results Page) analysis.

Ubersuggest, created by Neil Patel, offers keyword ideas, search volume data, keyword difficulty scores, and competitive analysis. It's a user-friendly tool that's great for beginners.

Long-Tail Keywords

Long-tail keywords are longer, more specific keyword phrases that tend to have lower search volumes but higher conversion rates. These keywords often reflect a clear intent and can be easier to rank for compared to short, broad keywords. For example, while "running shoes" is a highly competitive short-tail keyword, "best running shoes for flat feet" is a long-tail keyword that is more specific and likely to attract users ready to make a purchase. Using tools like Google's autocomplete feature, Answer the Public, and keyword research tools mentioned above can help you discover valuable long-tail keywords.

Competitive Analysis

Analysing your competitors' keywords is a critical step in keyword research. By understanding which keywords are driving traffic to their sites, you can identify gaps in your own strategy and discover new opportunities. Tools like Ahrefs, SEMrush, and Moz allow you to perform competitive analysis by entering a competitor's URL and viewing the keywords they rank for, their search volume, and their ranking position. This insight can help you develop a strategy to compete effectively.

Once you have a list of potential keywords, the next step is to analyse their search volume and competition. High search volume indicates a keyword is popular, but it often comes with high competition, making it harder to rank for. Conversely, low competition keywords might have lower search volumes but can be easier to rank for. Aim to strike a balance by targeting a mix of high-volume, high-competition keywords and low-volume, low-competition keywords. Tools like Google Keyword Planner, Ahrefs, and SEMrush provide data on search volume and competition, helping you make informed decisions.

Semantic Search and Related Keywords

Semantic search refers to search engines' ability to understand the context and intent behind a query rather than just matching exact keywords. This advancement means that related keywords and phrases also play a crucial role in SEO. Identify related keywords using tools like LSIGraph, which generates Latent Semantic Indexing (LSI) keywords that are semantically related to your primary keyword. Google's "People also ask" and "Related searches" sections can also provide valuable insights into related queries and topics.

Seasonal and Trend-Based Keywords

Consider incorporating seasonal and trend-based keywords into your strategy. Tools like Google Trends allow you to see how search interest for particular keywords fluctuates over time, helping you capitalise on seasonal trends and timely topics. For example, searches for "Christmas gift ideas" spike in the months leading up to December, while "best running shoes" might see a surge in the spring and early summer. Aligning your content strategy with these trends can drive significant traffic during peak periods.

Local SEO Keywords

For businesses that operate in specific geographic areas, local SEO keywords are essential. These keywords include location-specific terms that help attract local customers. Use tools like Google Business Profile, Moz Local, and BrightLocal to identify and optimise for local keywords. Incorporating local landmarks, neighbourhoods, and city names into your keywords can improve your visibility in local search results.

Monitoring and Refining Your Keyword Strategy

Keyword research is not a one-time task; it's an ongoing process that requires regular monitoring and refinement. Use tools like Google Analytics and Google Search Console to track the performance of your keywords and identify opportunities for improvement. Analyse metrics such as organic traffic, bounce rates, and conversion rates to determine which keywords are driving the most value. Continuously refine your keyword strategy based on this data to stay ahead of the competition and adapt to changes in search behaviour.

Keyword identification and analysis are essential to developing a robust and effective SEO strategy. By leveraging a combination of tools and techniques, you can uncover valuable keywords that align with your audience's search behaviour and intent. This comprehensive approach not only enhances your visibility in search engine results but also drives meaningful engagement and conversions. Remember, the landscape of SEO is constantly evolving, and staying informed and adaptable is key to sustained success.

Long-Tail vs. Short-Tail Keywords

Understanding the distinction between long-tail and short-tail keywords is fundamental to crafting a well-rounded SEO strategy. Each type of keyword serves different purposes and offers unique advantages, which can be leveraged to meet your specific business objectives. This section explores the characteristics, benefits, and strategic uses of long-tail and short-tail keywords, helping you to maximise your search engine optimisation efforts.

Short-tail keywords, also known as head terms, are broad search queries typically consisting of one to two words. Examples include "shoes," "marketing," or "SEO." These keywords are often highly competitive due to their broad nature and high search volumes. They are general in scope and can attract a wide range of searchers with varied intents.

However, the broadness of short-tail keywords can be both an advantage and a disadvantage. While they can drive a significant amount of traffic to your site, this traffic may not always be highly targeted, leading to lower conversion rates. Users searching for short-tail keywords may be at different stages of the buying journey, from initial research to ready-to-purchase, making it challenging to cater to their specific needs with general content.

Long-tail keywords, on the other hand, are more specific and often consist of three or more words. Examples include "best running shoes for flat feet," "digital marketing strategy for small businesses," or "how to improve SEO rankings." These keywords are less competitive and have lower search volumes compared to short-tail keywords. However, they attract a more targeted audience with a clearer search intent, often leading to higher conversion rates.

The specificity of long-tail keywords allows you to cater to niche audiences and address particular pain points or questions. Users searching with long-tail keywords typically have a more defined intent, whether they are looking for specific products, detailed information, or solutions to their problems. This specificity makes long-tail keywords incredibly valuable for driving qualified traffic and achieving better engagement and conversion rates.

Despite their broad nature, short-tail keywords offer several benefits. They are crucial for building brand awareness, especially for new websites or businesses looking to establish a presence in the digital landscape. Ranking for popular short-tail keywords can significantly increase your website's visibility and attract a large volume of traffic.

Additionally, short-tail keywords are often the foundation of a keyword strategy. They help identify broader topics around which you can create content, and they serve as a starting point for generating long-tail keyword variations. Optimising for short-tail keywords can also help improve your site's overall authority, as search engines recognise your relevance in key industry areas.

Long-tail keywords are essential for capturing highly targeted traffic and improving conversion rates. Because these keywords are more specific, they align closely with the user's search intent, making it easier to meet their needs and encourage engagement. Content optimised for long-tail keywords tends to perform better in terms of user satisfaction, as it provides precise answers and solutions.

Long-tail keywords also offer a competitive advantage. Due to their lower competition, it is generally easier to achieve higher rankings in search engine results pages (SERPs). This makes long-tail keywords particularly beneficial for small businesses or new websites that may struggle to compete for highly competitive short-tail keywords. Moreover, long-tail keywords often result in better user engagement metrics, such as lower bounce rates and higher time-on-page, which can positively influence your overall SEO performance.

A balanced SEO strategy incorporates both short-tail and long-tail keywords to achieve comprehensive coverage and maximise traffic potential. Here's how to strategically use each type:

Use short-tail keywords to build broad content pillars that cover general industry topics. These pillars can serve as the foundation for more detailed, long-tail keyword-targeted content. For instance, a short-tail keyword like "digital marketing" can be the basis for creating various in-depth articles on specific aspects of digital marketing, such as SEO, social media marketing, and email marketing.

Incorporate short-tail keywords into your site's main pages, such as the homepage, category pages, and main service pages. These keywords help establish your site's authority and relevance in your industry.

Develop detailed, niche content that addresses specific questions or problems using long-tail keywords. This approach can include blog posts, how-to guides, case studies, and product reviews. For example, a long-tail keyword like "how to improve SEO rankings for small businesses" can be the focus of a comprehensive guide that provides actionable tips and insights. However do NOT just stuff your website with FAQs for every question you can find because Google will now detect this.

Use long-tail keywords to optimise landing pages designed for specific campaigns or promotions. These pages can be highly targeted to match the exact needs of your audience, resulting in better conversion rates.

Employ long-tail keywords in your content marketing efforts to attract a more engaged audience. Creating content that answers specific queries can help you capture search traffic from users further along in the buying journey, who are more likely to convert.

Analysing Keyword Performance

Regularly analyse the performance of both short-tail and long-tail keywords to refine your strategy. Use tools like Google Search Console, SEMrush and other third-party SEO tools to track metrics such as search volume, click-through rates (CTR), and conversion rates. Pay attention to user engagement metrics, such as bounce rates and time-on-page, to understand how well your content meets the needs of your audience.

Adjust your strategy based on performance data. If certain short-tail keywords are driving high traffic but low conversions, consider how you can better address the needs of that broad audience. Conversely, if long-tail keywords are driving high engagement but have low search volumes, look for ways to expand on those topics to attract more visitors.

The Importance of Intent in Keyword Strategy

One thing I have observed is that if people fall at the hurdle of understanding keyword intent, then working on SEO is usually *not* for them. Grasping keyword intent is critical for creating content that resonates with your audience and achieves your business goals. Without understanding why users are searching for certain terms, you cannot effectively meet their needs or drive meaningful engagement.

When developing your keyword strategy, always consider the underlying intent behind each keyword. This will help you create content that not only ranks well but also provides real value to your audience, fostering trust and loyalty.

The strategic use of both long-tail and short-tail keywords is essential for a robust SEO strategy. By understanding the unique advantages and applications of each, you can create a well-rounded approach that drives traffic, engages users, and achieves high conversion rates. Remember, keyword research and optimisation are ongoing processes that require regular analysis and adaptation to stay ahead in the ever-evolving landscape of search engine optimisation.

CHAPTER 10

WRITING FOR SEO, READABILITY AND ENGAGEMENT

Writing for SEO *and* users' ability to absorb your content is a delicate balancing act that requires both technical precision and a deep understanding of user behaviour. It's not just about stuffing keywords into your content; it's about creating valuable, engaging, and easy-to-read content that also satisfies search engine algorithms. In this section, we'll explore the strategies and techniques to master this balance, ensuring that your content performs well both in search rankings and with your audience.

Understanding the Dual Goals: SEO and Readability

The primary goal of writing for SEO is to enhance your content's visibility on search engines, making it easier for potential customers to find you. This involves using targeted keywords, optimising meta elements, and ensuring your content is aligned with search engine algorithms. However, achieving high rankings alone isn't enough; your content must also be engaging and readable to keep visitors on your page and encourage them to take action.

Readability is about making your content accessible and enjoyable for your audience. This includes clear and concise writing, logical structure, and the use of visuals to break up text. Readable content improves user experience, reduces bounce rates, and increases the likelihood of conversions.

Integrating Keywords Naturally

One of the core principles of writing for SEO is the natural integration of keywords. Gone are the days of keyword stuffing, where cramming as many keywords into your content as possible was the norm. Today, search engines prioritise user experience, and overusing keywords can lead to penalties.

Instead, focus on incorporating keywords in a way that feels organic. This starts with thorough keyword research to identify relevant terms and phrases. Once you have your keywords, strategically place them in key areas such as:

Title Tags: Your main keyword should appear in the title tag, as this is one of the most important on-page SEO elements.

Headings and Subheadings: Use keywords in H1, H2, and H3 tags to structure your content and signal to search engines what your page is about.

Introduction: Mention your main keyword early in the introduction to immediately establish the topic.

Body Text: Disperse keywords naturally throughout the content. Aim for a keyword density of around 1-2%, ensuring they fit seamlessly into the narrative.

Meta Descriptions: Include your primary keyword in the meta description to improve click-through rates from SERPs.

Remember, the goal is to enhance the content's relevance without compromising readability. Always prioritise the reader's experience.

Crafting Engaging and Readable Content

Readable content is clear, concise, and engaging. Here are key strategies to improve readability:

Use Short Sentences and Paragraphs: Long sentences and dense paragraphs can overwhelm readers. Break up your content into short, digestible chunks to maintain reader interest.

Incorporate Subheadings: Subheadings not only help with SEO but also make your content easier to navigate. They allow readers to quickly scan and find the information they're looking for.

Bullet Points and Lists: Use bullet points and numbered lists to present information clearly and concisely. This format is easier for readers to digest and helps break up text.

Visuals and Multimedia: Include images, infographics, videos, and other multimedia elements to enhance your content. Visuals can make complex information more understandable and keep readers engaged.

Active Voice: Write in the active voice to make your content more direct and dynamic. Active voice sentences are typically shorter and clearer than passive voice sentences.

Simple Language: Avoid jargon and complex language. Write as if you're explaining something to a friend. Simple language ensures your content is accessible to a broader audience.

Storytelling: Incorporate storytelling elements to make your content more engaging. Stories help illustrate points and make information more memorable.

Consistent Tone and Style: Maintain a consistent tone and style throughout your content. Whether it's professional, casual, or somewhere in between, consistency helps build trust with your audience.

SEO Best Practices for Content Writing

Following SEO best practices ensures your content is not only engaging but also optimised for search engines. Here are some essential practices:

Optimise for Featured Snippets: Aim to answer common questions concisely and directly within your content. Featured snippets appear at the top of search results and can drive significant traffic.

Internal Linking: Use internal links to connect related content on your site. This helps search engines understand your site structure and keeps visitors engaged longer by guiding them to more information.

External Linking: Link to reputable external sources to back up your claims and provide additional value to your readers. This can also improve your content's credibility.

Mobile Optimisation: Ensure your content is mobile-friendly. With more users accessing content on mobile devices, a responsive design is crucial for maintaining readability and SEO performance.

Page Speed: Optimise your page load times. Slow-loading pages can negatively impact user experience and search rankings. Compress images, leverage browser caching, and minimise unnecessary code to improve speed.

Alt Text for Images: Use descriptive alt text for images. This not only helps with SEO but also improves accessibility for users with visual impairments.

Regular Updates: Keep your content up-to-date. Regularly review and update old content to ensure it remains relevant and accurate.

Using Data to Inform Your Writing

Leveraging data can significantly enhance both the SEO and readability of your content. Tools like Google Analytics, Google Search Console, and heatmaps can provide insights into how users interact with your content. Here's how to use this data effectively:

Identify High-Performing Content: Analyse which pages have the highest traffic, longest time on page, and best conversion rates. Use these pages as benchmarks for creating new content.

Understand User Behaviour: Heatmaps and session recordings can show you how users navigate your site, where they drop off, and which elements they interact with the most. Use this information to optimise content layout and structure.

Keyword Performance: Monitor how your target keywords are performing. Adjust your content strategy based on which keywords are driving traffic and conversions.

Engagement Metrics: Pay attention to metrics like bounce rate, time on page, and scroll depth. High bounce rates may indicate that your content isn't meeting user expectations, while deep scrolls and long time on page suggest high engagement.

A/B Testing: Conduct A/B tests on different content elements such as headlines, CTAs, and multimedia. Use the results to refine your content and improve user engagement.

Continuous Improvement and Adaptation

SEO and content writing are dynamic fields that require continuous learning and adaptation. Stay updated with the latest SEO trends and algorithm changes to ensure your content remains competitive. Engage with your audience through comments, social media, and feedback forms to understand their needs and preferences better.

Invest time in training and development to improve your writing skills and SEO knowledge. Attend webinars, read industry blogs, and participate in online courses to stay ahead of the curve.

Writing for SEO and readability is about creating content that not only ranks well in search engines but also engages and delights your audience. By integrating keywords naturally, crafting clear and compelling content, and following SEO best practices, you can achieve both goals effectively. Remember, the ultimate aim is to provide value to your readers while ensuring your content is easily discoverable by search engines. With continuous improvement and a focus on user experience, you can master the art of writing for SEO and readability, driving sustained traffic and engagement to your site.

Keep It Real

Have you ever worn the same thing as someone else to a party? Now imagine going to a party and realising over 100,000 people had the same idea. That's what happens when you write a blog post titled "How to optimise my blog post for SEO."

Original thought and compelling content are being drowned out by those who write just to rank, are too conservative, have no strategy, have little to say about their product, service, or industry, and are just plain lazy. Writing for SEO involves balancing technical precision with genuine, engaging content, but far too many brands are missing the mark.

Personally, I have a real problem with the overabundance of what's called "topic cluster content." This is pushed by the likes of HubSpot, the Content Marketing Institute, and many more. To explain this concept: you simply find your core topic (that people are searching for) and then you write more blog posts about related sub-topics (that people are searching for). The internet is being flooded by content that has absolutely no value. Content for the sake of content. And it must stop.

So, for example, if I were to write about how to optimise a blog post for SEO, then I might proceed to write a piece a week later about how to build relevant links to said blog post. Logical, right? Yes, but isn't it kind of boring?

Writing for SEO is okay to a point, but far too many brands are picking up on this technique and creating content that has little to no value. And it's sort of all the same. At best, it might be slightly useful – but it's probably been written over 100,000 times before. And much of it ends up in TL;DR territory.

Let's get to the point of what is considered to be poor-quality content, and then stay where you are so that we can discuss what to do about it.

According to Google's own guidelines, your content is of poor quality if it's lacking in purpose, harmful or offensive, presents unsubstantiated conspiracy theories, promotes hate or violence, is just a copy of an idea already present on the internet, or contains numerous grammatical errors or misspellings. And hidden somewhere within their documentation, if you look closely enough, there is also this key piece: little to no time, effort, expertise, manual curation, or added value for users. That's the real problem right there. They do not like lazy content.

Google has felt the need to create guidelines like EEAT (Experience, Expertise, Authoritativeness, Trustworthiness) because most people simply cannot follow their advice by writing with honesty and for the user.

The internet is being flooded and, over time, ruined by those creating content time and again that has absolutely no value. Content for the sake of content. And it must stop. The mere suggestion that you should have an opinion can be met with, "Yeah maybe if we were Ryanair or Paddy Power then we could get away with that." A knowing guffaw will usually follow. Well, guess what – those brands are getting away with it and it's getting them a lot of exposure. Their content is often original, has a supporting strategy, dares to create debate, and come on, they're having fun.

Brands who create content with honesty don't give much of a shit about what people are searching for, or what they will write about next week based on, well, what people are searching for again. They will write with authority, they will have an opinion, an original piece of thought, a tone of voice, a strategy – all of the core elements that are missing from most content.

The next time you sit down and strategise content, think about all of this. And very importantly, if you have a topic then Google it before you write so that you can ascertain if it's already been done a million times or not. And if it has then you'd better make it bloody good or else don't bother. Good content is not just storytelling, it's telling your story well.

And don't be afraid to have an opinion. If it doesn't work then life will go on (assuming you haven't said something completely ignorant or offensive). But you MUST have an opinion or a voice, or your content will not stand out. It just won't.

Furthermore, there are so many blogs that are chock full of articles about products or services and you've got to wonder why these are not just given a logical/permanent home on their website. Your blog is your place to have an opinion or a voice, not to shove a product benefit down someone's neck again. Let your product pages be great at doing that.

Don't focus on what everyone else is saying and then try to say it better. Instead, focus on trying to say what nobody has said yet. Now that's something of value. That's something I'll read. And so will many others.

We know that this is not easy. You do need to research your audiences, engage with them and better understand their needs. You need a direct line to those with the authority to greenlight and/or produce this content and have the opinion. You need the resources to produce something compelling.

So if you're wondering where to start with often limited resources, then look at your own industry – there are surely developments that you (or someone in your organisation) can have an opinion on. Everyone between four office walls has an opinion so be bold, back that up and talk about it. Read a lot. If you are not keeping pace with your industry then you may have an opinion that is outdated – or that someone has already had.

Do NOT always immediately look for what users are searching on Google for. Most searches do NOT end in a purchase, remember? Instead, use informed research and ask them what they'd like to see from you. Are there any industry experts who would be willing to write for you? They will be less afraid of judgment and might even have some credibility to lend. Weigh up the risks and rewards and maybe just do something cheap but fun.

With the right amount of effort and willingness, you'll not just be creating content that delights your audiences but also your audience's audiences. Now go and take risks with your content because the answer is always no if you're never even asked. Don't just be like the rest.

Importance of Content Quality and Relevance

Content is still king. Sorry, but it is. This adage has held true for years and continues to be a guiding principle for anyone serious about achieving success online. The quality and relevance of content are not just buzzwords; they are the foundation of effective SEO, user engagement, and ultimately, business growth. Let's delve into why content quality and relevance are so crucial and how you can ensure your content meets these essential criteria.

High-quality content is essential because it establishes trust and authority. In today's digital landscape, where misinformation and low-quality content abound, producing well-researched, accurate, and valuable content sets your brand apart as a credible source of information. When users consistently find useful and trustworthy information on your site, they are more likely to return, recommend your site to others, and convert into loyal customers. This trust not only fosters a positive relationship with your audience but also enhances your brand's reputation in the industry.

Relevance is equally important because it ensures that your content meets the specific needs and interests of your target audience. In a world where users are bombarded with information from all directions, delivering content that resonates with their particular pain points, questions, and desires is key to capturing and maintaining their attention. Relevant content is more likely to engage users, encourage interaction, and drive conversions because it addresses their immediate concerns and provides solutions that matter to them.

Moreover, the interplay between content quality and relevance has a significant impact on SEO. Search engines like Google prioritise content that provides value and is closely aligned with user intent. High-quality, relevant content is more likely to earn backlinks, social shares, and positive user signals, all of which are critical factors in search engine ranking algorithms. By focusing on quality and relevance, you can improve your website's visibility in search results, attract more organic traffic, and enhance your overall SEO performance.

To achieve high content quality, it's essential to invest in thorough research, meticulous editing, and professional presentation. This means understanding your subject matter deeply, presenting it clearly and compellingly, and ensuring that your content is free from errors and easy to read. Incorporating multimedia elements like images, videos, and infographics can also enhance the user experience and make your content more engaging.

Ensuring relevance involves a deep understanding of your audience. This requires continuous research to stay updated on their evolving needs, preferences, and behaviours. Using tools like Google Analytics, social media insights, and direct feedback from your audience can provide valuable data to inform your content strategy. By keeping a pulse on what your audience cares about, you can create content that is timely, pertinent, and valuable.

The quality and relevance of content are the cornerstones of effective digital marketing. They not only drive SEO success and user engagement but also contribute to building a trustworthy and authoritative brand. By prioritising these elements in your content strategy, you lay a solid foundation for sustained growth and success in the digital marketplace.

Content Quality: The Backbone of Effective SEO

When we talk about content quality, we're referring to more than just well-written text. Quality content is accurate, informative, engaging, and valuable to its intended audience. It requires time, effort, and expertise to create. Here's why it matters so much:

First and foremost, quality content builds trust with your audience. In an era where misinformation and low-quality content are rampant, providing reliable, well-researched information sets your brand apart as a credible source. When readers know they can depend on your content for accuracy and depth, they are more likely to return to your site, share your content with others, and become loyal followers or customers. Trust is a cornerstone of any successful relationship, and in the digital world, content is a key vehicle for building that trust.

Engagement is another critical aspect of quality content. Engaging content captivates the reader's attention, encouraging them to spend more time on your site, explore further, and interact with your content. This could mean anything from leaving a comment, sharing a post on social media, or clicking through to other pages on your site. High engagement rates are a positive signal to search engines, indicating that your content is valuable and relevant to users. This, in turn, can improve your search engine rankings, driving even more traffic to your site.

Valuable content also serves a practical purpose: it addresses the needs, questions, and pain points of your audience. Whether your audience is seeking solutions to specific problems, looking for detailed information on a topic, or simply wanting to be entertained, quality content delivers what they are looking for. This kind of value is what keeps people coming back to your site and encourages them to recommend your content to others. In a crowded digital space, providing real value is what helps your content stand out and gain traction.

Furthermore, quality content enhances your brand's authority and expertise in your industry. When you consistently produce content that is insightful, well-researched, and expertly crafted, you position your brand as a thought leader. This not only attracts more visitors but also opens up opportunities for partnerships, collaborations, and media attention. Being recognised as an authority in your field can have a profound impact on your business, leading to increased visibility and credibility.

Creating quality content also has long-term benefits for your SEO strategy. Search engines prioritise content that provides a great user experience, which includes factors like readability, relevance, and engagement. High-quality content is more likely to earn backlinks from other reputable sites, further boosting your SEO efforts. Additionally, quality content can help reduce bounce rates and increase dwell time, both of which are important metrics for search engine algorithms.

Lastly, investing in quality content can significantly enhance your conversion rates. When your content effectively communicates the value of your products or services and addresses the concerns of potential customers, it helps move them through the sales funnel. Clear, compelling, and persuasive content can turn visitors into leads and leads into customers. By focusing on quality, you ensure that your content not only attracts visitors but also converts them into loyal customers.

Quality content is a multifaceted asset that plays a crucial role in building trust, driving engagement, providing value, establishing authority, boosting SEO, and enhancing conversion rates. It requires dedication and expertise to create, but the benefits it brings to your digital marketing efforts are well worth the investment. By prioritising quality in your content strategy, you set the stage for sustainable growth and success in the digital landscape.

User Experience and Engagement

High-quality content enhances user experience, keeping visitors on your site longer and reducing bounce rates. Engaging content encourages users to explore more pages, interact with your site, and return in the future. This positive user behaviour sends strong signals to search engines, indicating that your site is valuable and worth ranking higher.

When we talk about enhancing user experience, it goes beyond just presenting information. It's about creating an immersive and intuitive journey that captivates the audience. High-quality content is meticulously crafted to be both informative and engaging, ensuring that it meets the needs and expectations of the audience. This involves using a clear, conversational tone, incorporating multimedia elements like images, videos, and infographics, and ensuring the content is easily navigable with a logical structure and internal linking.

A significant aspect of user engagement is the time users spend on your site, also known as dwell time. When users find your content valuable and engaging, they are more likely to stay on your site for extended periods. This prolonged engagement not only reduces bounce rates but also increases the chances of users exploring other pages on your site. Google and other search engines monitor these behaviours closely. A longer dwell time indicates to search engines that users find the content relevant and useful, which can positively impact your rankings.

Bounce rate, on the other hand, refers to the percentage of visitors who leave your site after viewing only one page. A high bounce rate often signals to search engines that your content did not meet the user's expectations or that the user experience was poor. Conversely, when users engage with your content and click through to other pages on your site, it shows that they find your site valuable and worth exploring further. Reducing bounce rates by providing high-quality, engaging content is crucial for improving your site's overall SEO performance.

Engaging content also encourages interactions. This can include leaving comments, sharing content on social media, and clicking on links to other parts of your site. These interactions not only enhance the user experience but also contribute to the overall visibility of your content. Social shares, in particular, can amplify your reach and attract a broader audience. The more your content is shared and discussed, the more authoritative it appears, which can further boost your rankings.

Furthermore, the return rate of visitors is another critical metric. When users repeatedly come back to your site, it signals to search engines that your content is consistently valuable and reliable. This loyalty builds a solid foundation for your site's authority and trustworthiness. High-quality content that resonates with your audience ensures that they return for more, establishing a strong relationship between your brand and your users.

Google's algorithms are designed to interpret these engagement metrics as indicators of content quality. For instance, RankBrain, Google's AI-based algorithm, is adept at understanding and evaluating user satisfaction. It looks at metrics like click-through rate (CTR), dwell time, and bounce rate to determine how well a piece of content meets the user's intent. Content that keeps users engaged is likely to perform better in search rankings because it aligns with Google's goal of providing the most relevant and useful results to its users.

In addition to these metrics, user feedback also plays a role. When users bookmark your site, leave positive reviews, or refer others to your content, it creates a ripple effect that enhances your site's credibility and authority. These actions are tracked and considered by search engines as part of their ranking algorithms. The more positive signals your content generates, the higher it is likely to rank.

Moreover, high-quality content fosters trust and builds a loyal audience. When users trust the information you provide, they are more likely to recommend your site to others, increasing your organic traffic and further solidifying your authority in your niche. This trust is built over time through consistent delivery of valuable and accurate content that meets the evolving needs of your audience.

In summary, the creation of high-quality content is integral to enhancing user experience, driving engagement, and signalling value to search engines. By keeping visitors on your site longer, reducing bounce rates, and encouraging interaction, you send strong positive signals to search engines, indicating that your site is valuable and deserving of higher rankings. This holistic approach to content creation not only boosts your SEO performance but also fosters a loyal and engaged audience, laying the groundwork for sustained success in the digital landscape.

Trust and Authority

Creating accurate, well-researched content establishes your brand as an authority in your industry. When users find reliable information on your site, they are more likely to trust your brand and become loyal customers. Search engines like Google reward sites that demonstrate expertise, authority, and trustworthiness (E-E-A-T), further boosting your rankings.

Accurate, well-researched content is the backbone of a successful digital presence. It involves a meticulous process of gathering, verifying, and presenting information that is not only correct but also insightful and valuable to your audience. This commitment to accuracy reflects a dedication to quality that users appreciate and trust. When your content consistently provides precise and well-supported information, it builds a reputation for reliability that distinguishes your brand in a crowded marketplace.

Establishing authority through high-quality content involves demonstrating a deep understanding of your industry. This means staying current with the latest developments, trends, and best practices. By incorporating up-to-date research, expert opinions, and data-driven insights into your content, you position your brand as a knowledgeable leader. This authoritative stance is crucial for building credibility with your audience, as users are more likely to trust and engage with content that is backed by expertise.

The role of expertise in content creation cannot be overstated. Expertise ensures that the information provided is not only accurate but also relevant and actionable. When users encounter content that addresses their needs with precision and depth, they recognise the value of the expertise behind it. This recognition fosters trust, encouraging users to return to your site for future information needs. Over time, this repeated engagement helps solidify your brand's position as an authoritative source within your industry.

Trustworthiness is another critical element that underpins effective content. Users must feel confident that the information they are consuming is trustworthy and unbiased. This trust is built through transparency, consistency, and a demonstrated commitment to providing value. Transparent content practices, such as citing sources, acknowledging potential biases, and providing balanced perspectives, help establish a foundation of trust. Consistently delivering high-quality content that meets user expectations further reinforces this trust, making users more likely to become loyal advocates for your brand.

Search engines like Google place a high premium on E-E-A-T (Expertise, Authoritativeness, Trustworthiness) when evaluating content.

These principles are embedded in Google's algorithms, which assess the quality of content based on the expertise of the authors, the authoritativeness of the content, and the trustworthiness of the site as a whole. Sites that excel in these areas are more likely to achieve higher rankings in search results, as Google aims to provide users with the most reliable and valuable information available.

Demonstrating expertise through content involves showcasing the qualifications and experience of your authors. This can be achieved by highlighting their credentials, professional backgrounds, and relevant accomplishments. By clearly communicating the expertise behind your content, you enhance its credibility and appeal to both users and search engines. Author bios, expert interviews, and guest contributions from industry leaders are effective strategies for conveying expertise.

Authoritativeness is reinforced through comprehensive, in-depth content that thoroughly addresses the topics at hand. This includes providing detailed explanations, supporting arguments with evidence, and exploring various facets of a subject. Authoritative content goes beyond surface-level information, offering valuable insights that help users make informed decisions. By consistently producing authoritative content, your brand becomes a go-to resource for reliable information, further solidifying your position in the industry.

Trustworthiness is cultivated through ethical content practices and a user-centric approach. This involves prioritising the needs and interests of your audience, rather than solely focusing on SEO or promotional goals. Providing balanced, unbiased information, being transparent about affiliations and sponsorships, and respecting user privacy are all essential components of trustworthy content. When users perceive your content as trustworthy, they are more likely to engage with it, share it, and recommend your brand to others.

The impact of E-E-A-T on search rankings is significant. Google's algorithms are designed to prioritise content that demonstrates a high level of expertise, authoritativeness, and trustworthiness. This means that sites that consistently produce high-quality, accurate, and well-researched content are more likely to achieve and maintain prominent positions in search results. This visibility not only drives organic traffic but also enhances brand recognition and credibility.

Moreover, the benefits of creating accurate, well-researched content extend beyond search rankings. High-quality content fosters deeper user engagement, encouraging visitors to spend more time on your site, explore additional pages, and interact with your brand. This engagement signals to search engines that your site is valuable and relevant, further boosting your SEO performance. Additionally, satisfied users are more likely to convert into loyal customers, subscribe to your newsletters, and share your content with their networks, amplifying your reach and influence.

Creating accurate, well-researched content is essential for establishing your brand as an authority in your industry. It builds trust and loyalty among your audience, enhances user engagement, and aligns with Google's E-E-A-T guidelines to boost your search rankings. By investing in high-quality content that demonstrates expertise, authoritativeness, and trustworthiness, you lay the foundation for sustained success in the digital landscape. This strategic approach not only elevates your brand's visibility but also fosters meaningful connections with your audience, driving long-term growth and profitability.

SEO Performance

Quality content is integral to SEO. Search engines use complex algorithms to evaluate the quality of content. They look for factors like original research, depth of information, proper grammar, and user satisfaction. Pages with high-quality content are more likely to rank well in search results, attract backlinks, and gain social shares, all of which enhance SEO performance.

When we talk about the importance of quality content, it's essential to understand that search engines like Google have become increasingly sophisticated. Gone are the days when simply stuffing a page with keywords could propel it to the top of search results. Today, search engines utilise advanced algorithms designed to mimic human evaluation of content quality. This involves a nuanced understanding of various factors that contribute to content excellence.

One of the primary aspects search engines consider is original research. In an age where information is abundant, the value of unique, original content cannot be overstated. Original research demonstrates a commitment to providing fresh and valuable insights that users cannot find elsewhere. It distinguishes your content from the plethora of repetitive and derivative articles that flood the internet. Search engines reward this originality because it aligns with their goal of delivering the most relevant and informative results to users. Consequently, content that incorporates original research is more likely to be indexed favourably, enhancing its visibility and reach.

Depth of information is another crucial criterion. Surface-level content that barely scratches the topic's surface is unlikely to satisfy users' needs or earn a prominent spot in search results. Comprehensive content that delves deeply into a subject, exploring various facets and providing detailed analysis, is far more effective. This depth not only helps to address a wide range of user queries but also signals to search engines that the content is thorough and valuable. In-depth articles are often perceived as more authoritative and credible, qualities that search engines prioritise in their rankings.

Proper grammar and readability play significant roles in content quality. While they might seem basic, these elements are fundamental to user experience. Content riddled with grammatical errors and poorly constructed sentences is difficult to read and can frustrate users, leading to higher bounce rates. Search engines track user engagement metrics, such as time spent on a page and bounce rates, to gauge content quality. Well-written, grammatically sound content is easier to read and understand, encouraging users to stay longer on the page and explore additional content. This positive user behaviour can lead to higher rankings and improved SEO performance.

User satisfaction is the ultimate goal of search engines, and it is closely tied to content quality. Search engines strive to deliver content that meets users' needs and provides a satisfying experience. Various factors contribute to user satisfaction, including the relevance of the content to the user's query, the ease of navigation, the speed of the website, and the overall presentation of the content. When users find content that answers their questions thoroughly and efficiently, they are more likely to engage with it, share it, and return to the site in the future. These actions send strong positive signals to search engines, reinforcing the content's value and boosting its ranking potential.

High-quality content also has a propensity to attract backlinks, which are crucial for SEO. Backlinks, or inbound links, are links from other websites to your content. They act as endorsements, signalling to search engines that your content is credible and valuable. Quality content that offers unique insights, thorough analysis, or practical solutions is more likely to be referenced by other websites. These backlinks not only drive referral traffic but also enhance your site's authority in the eyes of search engines, leading to higher rankings.

Furthermore, quality content is more likely to gain social shares. In today's interconnected digital landscape, social media plays a pivotal role in content dissemination. Engaging, informative, and well-crafted content resonates with audiences and encourages them to share it across social media platforms. These shares increase the content's reach, driving more traffic to your site and amplifying its impact. While social shares themselves may not directly influence search rankings, the increased visibility and traffic they generate can lead to more backlinks and enhanced user engagement, both of which positively affect SEO.

Search engines are continuously refining their algorithms to better assess content quality. Innovations such as natural language processing (NLP) and machine learning enable search engines to understand the context and semantics of content more effectively. These advancements mean that search engines are becoming adept at evaluating the overall value of content, considering factors such as coherence, relevance, and the presence of structured data. High-quality content that aligns with these evolving criteria is better positioned to perform well in search rankings.

To ensure your content meets these high standards, consider the following strategies. First, prioritise thorough research and fact-checking to ensure accuracy and reliability. Invest time in understanding your audience's needs and preferences to create content that resonates with them. Use clear, concise, and engaging language to enhance readability and user experience. Incorporate multimedia elements, such as images, videos, and infographics, to enrich the content and cater to different learning styles. Finally, regularly update your content to keep it current and relevant, which signals to search engines that your site is active and continually providing value.

In summary, quality content is the cornerstone of effective SEO. By focusing on original research, depth of information, proper grammar, and user satisfaction, you can create content that not only ranks well in search results but also engages and retains users. This holistic approach to content creation ensures that your site remains competitive in the ever-evolving digital landscape, driving sustained growth and success.

I have meticulously combed through every section of Google's extensive (leaked) content rater guidelines, as used by their own internal teams. Given its substantial length, I aim to save you time by summarising the key points here in my own words. While some points may echo previous discussions, this summary is designed to be a handy reference for you...

Google's Own Internal Search Quality Evaluator Guidelines; A Crude Summary

The Google Search Quality Evaluator Guidelines provide a comprehensive framework for evaluating the quality of web pages and their relevance to search queries. These guidelines are essential for ensuring that Google's search results meet user needs by prioritising high-quality, reliable, and useful content. Below is a detailed summary of the guidelines, structured to highlight the key components and their importance in the search evaluation process when performed by **actual humans.**

Purpose of Search Quality Rating: The primary goal is to evaluate how well Google's search results meet the needs of users across different languages and locales. Ratings provided by quality evaluators do not directly affect page rankings but help improve the algorithms that determine search rankings.

Role of Raters: Raters are tasked with evaluating the quality and relevance of search results based on the guidelines. They must represent the users in their locale and base their ratings on the instructions and examples provided, not personal opinions.

Understanding Webpages and Websites: Raters need to understand the structure and purpose of web pages and websites. This includes identifying the main content (MC), supplementary content (SC), and advertisements (Ads).

Identifying the Purpose of a Webpage: Every webpage is created with a purpose, which can range from sharing information, expressing opinions, selling products, to providing entertainment. Understanding this purpose is crucial for accurate PQ rating.

Your Money or Your Life (YMYL) Pages: YMYL pages are those that can significantly impact a person's health, financial stability, or safety. These pages require higher standards of accuracy and trustworthiness.

Main Content (MC): This is the primary information on the page that helps achieve the page's purpose. High-quality MC is a critical factor in PQ rating.

Supplementary Content (SC): SC enhances user experience but does not directly help achieve the page's purpose. Examples include navigation links and sidebars.

Advertisements (Ads): Ads are for monetising the page. While necessary for many websites, excessive or intrusive ads can negatively impact page quality.

Experience, Expertise, Authoritativeness, and Trustworthiness (E-E-A-T): Pages should demonstrate a high level of E-E-A-T, particularly for YMYL topics. This involves showing that the content creator has relevant experience and expertise, the website is authoritative, and the information is trustworthy.

Reputation of the Website and Content Creators: Evaluators need to assess the reputation of the website and its content creators through independent sources, such as user reviews and references.

Lowest Quality Pages: Pages that spread hate, cause harm, or deceive users should be rated as the lowest quality. These include pages with malicious behaviour, spam, or those that deliberately mislead users.

Low Quality Pages: Pages with low E-E-A-T, inadequate MC, or those that disrupt the user experience with distracting ads or SC are considered low quality.

High Quality Pages: These pages have excellent MC, a positive reputation, and demonstrate a high level of E-E-A-T. They provide a satisfying amount of high-quality content and useful supplementary content.

Highest Quality Pages: These pages exceed expectations in all PQ aspects. They provide exceptional content, a very positive reputation, and the highest level of E-E-A-T.

Understanding Search User Needs: Evaluators must understand the intent behind user queries to accurately assess how well search results meet those needs. This includes considering different types of queries, such as informational, transactional, and navigational.

Rating Scale: The Needs Met rating scale ranges from "Fully Meets" to "Fails to Meet." It measures how well the search result satisfies the user's intent and query.

These guidelines are designed to ensure that search results are helpful, relevant, and trustworthy. By adhering to these guidelines, quality raters play a crucial role in refining the algorithms that power Google's search engine, ultimately enhancing the user experience by delivering higher quality content.

While quality is vital, relevance is equally important. Content must align with the needs and interests of your target audience. Relevant content answers users' questions, solves their problems, and meets their search intent. Here's why relevance is critical:

Understanding and addressing search intent is paramount. Users come to your site with specific needs, whether informational, navigational, transactional, or investigational. Content that directly satisfies these needs leads to higher user satisfaction, better engagement, and improved conversion rates.

Relevance involves aligning your content with the right topics that your audience is searching for. This requires thorough keyword research and an understanding of your audience's search behaviour. By using relevant keywords naturally within high-quality content, you increase your chances of ranking well and attracting organic traffic.

Relevance also means providing contextually appropriate content tailored to different stages of the buyer's journey. Personalised content that resonates with users' current needs and preferences fosters deeper connections and enhances the likelihood of conversions.

How to Ensure Content Quality and Relevance

Ensuring your content is both high-quality and relevant involves several key practices:

In-Depth Research

Thorough research is the cornerstone of quality content. This includes understanding your audience, conducting keyword research, and staying updated on industry trends. Use tools like Google Analytics, SEMrush, and social listening platforms to gather insights.

Originality and Uniqueness: Avoid regurgitating information that's already available. Provide unique insights, original research, and fresh perspectives. This not only sets your content apart but also adds value to your audience.

Clarity and Readability: Ensure your content is easy to read and understand. Use clear language, short paragraphs, subheadings, bullet points, and visuals to break up text. Tools like Hemingway Editor and Grammarly can help improve readability and catch grammatical errors.

Engagement and Interaction: Incorporate interactive elements like quizzes, polls, videos, and infographics to engage your audience. Encourage comments, shares, and feedback to foster a sense of community and interaction.

Regular Updates: Content relevance can diminish over time. Regularly update your content to ensure it remains accurate and relevant. This shows search engines and users that your site is maintained and trustworthy.

User Feedback: Pay attention to user feedback and analytics. High bounce rates or low engagement might indicate that your content isn't meeting user expectations. Use this data to refine and improve your content strategy.

Cross-Platform Consistency: Ensure your content is consistent across all platforms, whether it's your website, social media, or email newsletters. Consistency helps build brand recognition and trust.

The Real-World Impact of Quality and Relevance

Consider the difference between a blog that churns out keyword-stuffed, low-value articles and one that produces thoughtful, well-researched content. The former might see a temporary spike in traffic, but users quickly leave, resulting in high bounce rates and poor engagement metrics. The latter, however, attracts a loyal audience, gains valuable backlinks, and enjoys sustained organic traffic growth.

For instance, a company that invests in high-quality, relevant content might find that their articles get shared more often, cited by other authoritative sources, and ranked higher in search engine results. This not only drives more traffic but also positions the company as a leader in its field.

The importance of content quality and relevance cannot be overstated. They are the bedrock of effective SEO, driving user engagement, building trust, and ensuring sustained business success. By committing to creating high-quality, relevant content, you not only enhance your SEO performance but also deliver real value to your audience.

This commitment to excellence in content creation will set you apart in a crowded digital landscape, ensuring that your brand not only attracts but also retains a loyal and engaged audience. As you move forward, remember that the time and effort invested in creating quality, relevant content will pay dividends in the form of higher rankings, increased traffic, and greater user satisfaction.

CHAPTER 11
CONTENT FORMATS AND MULTIMEDIA SEO

Content is not limited to text. Obviously. The evolution of the internet has brought about diverse content formats, including videos, images, and voice. These different formats cater to varied user preferences and enhance user engagement. This chapter delves into the significance of various content formats and provides comprehensive strategies for optimising non-text content for SEO, ensuring your content stands out in search results and reaches your target audience effectively.

As the internet has grown and evolved, so have the ways in which we consume information. No longer are we limited to reading text on a screen; now we can watch videos, view images, and even listen to content through voice-enabled devices. This diversification of content formats has been driven by technological advancements, changing user behaviours, and the need for more engaging and accessible ways to convey information. Each format offers unique advantages and challenges, and understanding how to leverage them can significantly impact your digital marketing success.

Video content has become one of the most powerful tools in digital marketing. Platforms like YouTube, Vimeo, and social media channels such as Facebook, Instagram, and TikTok have made video a central part of the online experience. Videos can explain complex topics in an easily digestible format, demonstrate products in action, and create emotional connections with viewers. They cater to the increasing demand for visual content and the preference for consuming information quickly and efficiently.

Optimising video content for SEO involves several key strategies. First, it's essential to create high-quality, relevant videos that address the needs and interests of your target audience. Use descriptive titles, tags, and detailed descriptions with relevant keywords to help search engines understand the content of your videos. Adding transcripts and subtitles can enhance accessibility and improve SEO by providing additional text for search engines to crawl. Thumbnails should be visually appealing and relevant to the video content, as they are the first thing users see and can significantly influence click-through rates.

Images are another crucial element of digital content. They can capture attention, convey messages quickly, and break up text to make content more visually appealing. High-quality images can enhance blog posts, social media updates, product pages, and more. In industries like fashion, travel, food, and real estate, compelling visuals are essential for engaging users and driving conversions.

To optimise images for SEO, use descriptive, keyword-rich file names and alt text to help search engines understand the content of your images. Alt text also improves accessibility for visually impaired users who rely on screen readers. Compress images to reduce file size without sacrificing quality, ensuring faster page load times and a better user experience. Use responsive images that adjust to different screen sizes to maintain visual quality across devices.

Voice search and voice-activated content are rapidly gaining popularity, driven by the proliferation of smart speakers and virtual assistants like Amazon Alexa, Google Assistant, and Apple's Siri. Voice content offers a hands-free, convenient way for users to access information, making it an essential component of a modern digital strategy.

Optimising for voice search requires a different approach than traditional text-based SEO. Voice searches tend to be more conversational and question-based, so focus on natural language keywords and phrases. Creating FAQ pages and optimising content for featured snippets can increase the likelihood of your content being used in voice search results. Additionally, ensure your website is mobile-friendly and has fast load times, as many voice searches are conducted on mobile devices.

Integrating a mix of content formats into your digital strategy can significantly enhance user engagement and SEO performance. Each format caters to different user preferences and can be used to complement and reinforce your overall content strategy. For example, a blog post can be accompanied by an engaging video, relevant images, and a downloadable podcast episode. This multi-format approach ensures that your content reaches a broader audience and provides multiple touchpoints for engagement.

Regularly monitoring the performance of your multimedia content is crucial for understanding what resonates with your audience and optimising your strategy accordingly. Use analytics tools to track metrics such as views, engagement, click-through rates, and conversions. These insights can help you identify which formats and topics are most effective, allowing you to refine your content strategy and achieve better results.

The digital landscape is constantly evolving, and staying updated with the latest trends and best practices is essential for maintaining a competitive edge. Follow industry blogs, participate in webinars, and attend conferences to keep abreast of new developments in content formats and SEO. This proactive approach will help you adapt to changes and continue to deliver high-quality, relevant content that meets the needs of your audience.

The diversification of content formats presents a wealth of opportunities for digital marketers. By embracing videos, images, and voice content and optimising each format for SEO, you can create a comprehensive and engaging digital strategy that appeals to a wide range of users. This approach not only enhances user experience but also improves your site's visibility and ranking in search results, driving traffic and achieving your business goals.

Content Formats: Video, Images, Text, and Voice

The digital age has revolutionised the way content is consumed. Different formats of content cater to diverse user preferences, making it imperative for digital marketers to incorporate a variety of content types into their strategies. Understanding the unique advantages and challenges of each content format can significantly enhance your ability to engage with your audience, improve SEO performance, and achieve your marketing goals.

The Pervasiveness of Video Content

Video content has become a cornerstone of digital marketing, driven by the rapid growth of platforms like YouTube, TikTok, Instagram, and Facebook. The rise of video content is not just a trend but a response to the increasing demand for visual and interactive experiences. Videos can convey complex information in an engaging and easily digestible manner, making them an excellent tool for tutorials, product demonstrations, testimonials, and brand storytelling.

Moreover, the dynamic nature of video content captures attention more effectively than static images or text. Videos are more likely to be shared on social media, increasing your reach and potential for virality. To optimise video content for SEO, focus on creating high-quality videos that are relevant to your audience. Use compelling titles, descriptions, and tags enriched with relevant keywords to help search engines understand the content. Adding transcripts and subtitles not only improves accessibility but also provides additional text for search engines to crawl, enhancing your video's SEO value.

The Visual Impact of Images

Images play a crucial role in digital content by breaking up text, capturing attention, and conveying messages quickly. High-quality images can enhance the aesthetic appeal of your content, making it more engaging and shareable. In industries such as fashion, food, travel, and real estate, compelling visuals are essential for showcasing products and services effectively.

To optimise images for SEO, use descriptive file names and alt text that include relevant keywords. This helps search engines understand the content of the images, improving their visibility in image search results. Compressing images to reduce file size without compromising quality is crucial for maintaining fast page load times, which is a key factor in user experience and SEO. Additionally, using responsive images ensures that they display correctly across various devices, enhancing accessibility and user satisfaction.

The Timeless Relevance of Text

Despite the growing popularity of visual and audio content, text remains a fundamental component of digital marketing. Text content, including blog posts, articles, eBooks, and whitepapers, provides in-depth information and establishes authority on a subject. Well-written text content can drive organic traffic, generate leads, and build trust with your audience.

Creating high-quality text content involves thorough research, clear and engaging writing, and the strategic use of keywords. It's essential to address the needs and interests of your audience, providing valuable insights and solutions to their problems. Incorporating keywords naturally into your content helps search engines understand its relevance to specific queries, improving your chances of ranking higher in search results. Additionally, structuring your content with headings, subheadings, bullet points, and short paragraphs enhances readability and user engagement.

The Emergence of Voice Content

Voice content is rapidly gaining traction, thanks to the proliferation of smart speakers and virtual assistants like Amazon Alexa, Google Assistant, and Apple Siri. Voice search offers a hands-free, convenient way for users to access information, making it an increasingly important aspect of digital marketing strategies.

Optimising for voice search requires a different approach than traditional text-based SEO. Voice queries tend to be longer and more conversational, so it's important to focus on natural language keywords and phrases. Creating FAQ pages and optimising content for featured snippets can increase the likelihood of your content being used in voice search results. Ensuring your website is mobile-friendly and has fast load times is also crucial, as many voice searches are conducted on mobile devices.

Integrating Multiple Content Formats

An effective digital marketing strategy leverages a mix of content formats to cater to different user preferences and enhance overall engagement. Combining videos, images, text, and voice content allows you to reach a broader audience and provide a richer user experience. For example, a blog post can be accompanied by an instructional video, relevant images, and a downloadable podcast episode. This multi-format approach not only caters to varied consumption habits but also reinforces your message across different mediums.

Challenges and Best Practices

While incorporating diverse content formats offers numerous benefits, it also presents certain challenges. Each format requires a unique approach to creation, optimisation, and distribution. Ensuring consistency in your brand voice and message across different formats can be challenging but is essential for maintaining a cohesive brand identity.

Regularly updating and refreshing your content is also important to keep it relevant and engaging. Use analytics tools to track the performance of your content across different formats, identifying what works best for your audience. This data-driven approach allows you to refine your strategy and focus on the formats that drive the most engagement and conversions.

As technology continues to evolve, new content formats and platforms will emerge, offering fresh opportunities for digital marketers. Staying abreast of these trends and being willing to experiment with new formats will be crucial for maintaining a competitive edge. By embracing a diverse range of content formats and optimising each one for SEO, you can create a comprehensive and effective digital marketing strategy that resonates with your audience and drives long-term success.

Optimising Video Content

Videos have become an integral part of digital marketing, offering a dynamic way to engage audiences, convey complex information, and boost SEO efforts. However, simply creating video content is not enough; it must be meticulously optimised to maximise its impact on search engine rankings and user engagement. Here's how you can ensure your video content is effectively optimised for SEO:

Title and Description: The title and description of your video play a crucial role in its discoverability. Just as with blog posts and web pages, incorporating relevant keywords into your video title can significantly enhance its visibility in search results. A well-crafted title should be clear, compelling, and reflective of the video's content. For example, instead of a vague title like "How-To Video," opt for something more descriptive such as "How to Optimise Your Blog Posts for SEO: A Step-by-Step Guide." The video description is equally important. It should provide a concise yet informative overview of what the video is about. Including relevant keywords naturally within the description helps search engines understand the context of the video, making it more likely to appear in relevant search queries. Additionally, a good description should include a call to action (CTA), encouraging viewers to take the next step, whether it's subscribing to your channel, visiting your website, or engaging with your content in another way.

Transcripts and Subtitles: Adding transcripts and subtitles to your videos can significantly enhance their accessibility and SEO performance. Transcripts are a textual representation of the video's audio content, which can be indexed by search engines. This not only helps search engines understand the content of your video but also provides an opportunity to rank for additional keywords.

Subtitles and closed captions make your videos accessible to a broader audience, including those who are deaf or hard of hearing, non-native speakers, and users who prefer watching videos without sound. Platforms like YouTube and Facebook also index subtitles, which can further improve your video's SEO. Moreover, subtitles can enhance user experience by allowing viewers to follow along with the video even in noisy environments or situations where they can't use audio.

Thumbnails: Thumbnails are the first visual element that viewers see when they come across your video. A compelling and relevant thumbnail can significantly increase the click-through rate (CTR) of your video content. Thumbnails should be eye-catching, high-quality, and accurately represent the video's content. Avoid using clickbait thumbnails that mislead viewers, as this can lead to higher bounce rates and lower engagement. Custom thumbnails generally perform better than automatically generated ones. Creating a custom thumbnail that includes text overlays, branded elements, or engaging imagery can entice users to click and watch your video. The thumbnail should be designed with your audience in mind, considering what would most likely grab their attention and prompt them to engage with your content.

Embedding and Sharing: Embedding videos on your website and sharing them across social media platforms is crucial for increasing their reach and engagement. When embedding videos on your website, ensure the video player is responsive, meaning it adapts to different screen sizes and devices. A non-responsive video player can lead to a poor user experience, negatively impacting your SEO. Sharing your videos on social media platforms can amplify their reach, driving more traffic to your website and increasing overall engagement. Each social media platform has its own best practices for video content, so tailor your approach accordingly. For instance, shorter, attention-grabbing videos may perform better on platforms like Instagram and Twitter, while longer, more in-depth videos might be more suitable for YouTube and Facebook.

To maximise the SEO benefits of your embedded and shared videos, consider the following strategies:

Optimise the Video URL and Embedding Code: Use SEO-friendly URLs and embedding codes that include relevant keywords. This helps search engines understand the context of the video and improves its chances of ranking in search results.

Leverage Social Sharing Buttons: Make it easy for viewers to share your videos by including social sharing buttons on your website and video pages. Increased shares can lead to more views, higher engagement, and improved SEO.

Encourage Engagement: Prompt viewers to like, comment, and share your videos. Engagement metrics such as likes, comments, and shares signal to search engines that your content is valuable, which can positively impact your rankings.

Monitor Performance: Use analytics tools to track the performance of your videos. Platforms like YouTube provide detailed insights into viewer behaviour, including watch time, demographics, and engagement metrics. Use this data to refine your video strategy and optimise future content.

To further enhance the SEO of your video content, consider creating a video sitemap and implementing schema markup. A video sitemap is a specific type of XML sitemap that provides search engines with detailed information about the video content on your site. This includes metadata such as the video title, description, duration, and thumbnail URL. Submitting a video sitemap to search engines can improve the indexation and discoverability of your video content.

Schema markup, also known as structured data (as discussed in a previous chapter) provides additional context to search engines about the content of your video. By adding video schema markup to your HTML, you can help search engines better understand the video's content, leading to enhanced search listings. For example, videos with schema markup may appear in rich snippets, which are search results that include additional information like thumbnails, descriptions, and publication dates. This can increase your video's visibility and CTR.

Engagement and interaction are critical components of video SEO. Encouraging viewers to interact with your video content can enhance its performance and signal its value to search engines. Here are some ways to foster engagement:

Ask Questions: Prompt viewers to leave comments by asking questions or encouraging them to share their thoughts on the topic.

This can increase the number of comments and foster a sense of community around your content.

Use End Screens and Annotations: End screens and annotations can guide viewers to take specific actions, such as watching another video, subscribing to your channel, or visiting your website. These interactive elements can keep viewers engaged and drive additional traffic to your content.

Respond to Comments: Engaging with viewers in the comments section can build relationships and encourage further interaction. Responding to comments shows that you value viewer feedback and are actively participating in the conversation.

Run Contests and Giveaways: Contests and giveaways can incentivise viewers to engage with your video content. Encourage viewers to like, comment, and share your videos for a chance to win a prize. This can increase engagement and expand your video's reach.

Optimising video content is a multifaceted process that involves more than just creating high-quality videos. By focusing on titles, descriptions, transcripts, thumbnails, embedding, sharing, and engagement, you can maximise the SEO potential of your video content. Additionally, leveraging video sitemaps and schema markup can further enhance your video's visibility and discoverability in search results.

As the digital landscape continues to evolve, video content will remain a powerful tool for engaging audiences and driving SEO performance. By implementing these strategies and continuously refining your approach based on data and insights, you can ensure that your video content stands out in search results and effectively reaches your target audience.

Optimising Image Content

Images play a pivotal role in enhancing the visual appeal and user engagement of your website content. However, their benefits extend beyond aesthetics; properly optimised images can significantly boost your SEO performance. Here's an in-depth guide on how to optimise your images for maximum SEO impact.

Alt Text: Alt text, or alternative text, is a crucial component of image SEO. It serves multiple purposes, including improving accessibility for visually impaired users and helping search engines understand the content of your images. When crafting alt text, use descriptive and relevant keywords that accurately represent the image. Avoid keyword stuffing, as it can be counterproductive. Instead, focus on creating concise, meaningful descriptions that enhance the overall user experience. For example, instead of a generic alt text like "flower," use something more specific like "red rose in full bloom."

File Names: The file name of your image is another important factor in image optimisation. Before uploading an image, rename the file with a descriptive, keyword-rich name that reflects the content of the image. Search engines use file names to index and rank images, so incorporating relevant keywords can improve your image's search visibility. For instance, instead of a default file name like "IMG_1234.jpg," use a more descriptive name like "red-rose-flower.jpg." This practice not only aids in SEO but also makes file management more organised and intuitive.

Image Size and Compression: Image size and compression are critical for maintaining optimal page load times. Large, uncompressed images can significantly slow down your website, leading to a poor user experience and negatively impacting your SEO. To avoid this, resize your images to the appropriate dimensions needed for your website and compress them using tools like TinyPNG, JPEG Optimiser, or ImageOptim. These tools reduce the file size without compromising image quality, ensuring your pages load quickly and efficiently. Additionally, consider using modern image formats like WebP, which offer superior compression and quality compared to traditional formats like JPEG and PNG.

Captions and Context: Captions provide additional context and information about your images, enhancing user understanding and engagement. While captions are not directly used by search engines for ranking, they contribute to the overall content quality and user experience. When writing captions, ensure they are relevant, descriptive, and add value to the content. A well-crafted caption can attract attention, encourage users to spend more time on your page, and improve readability. For example, instead of a simple caption like "flower," use something more engaging like "A stunning red rose in full bloom, symbolising love and passion."

Image Placement and Relevance: The placement and relevance of images within your content also play a role in optimisation. Ensure that images are contextually relevant to the surrounding text and placed strategically to support and enhance the content. Images should not be used merely for decoration; they should provide visual support and clarification for the information presented. For example, if your article discusses the benefits of different types of roses, include images of each rose type next to their respective descriptions. This practice not only improves user engagement but also helps search engines understand the context and relevance of the images.

Creating an image sitemap can further enhance the discoverability of your images. An image sitemap is an XML file that provides search engines with information about the images on your website, including their location, title, caption, and license information. By submitting an image sitemap to search engines, you can ensure that all your images are indexed and included in image search results. This can drive additional traffic to your site from users searching for specific images. Use tools like Google's Image Sitemap Generator to create and submit your image sitemap.

In today's multi-device world, ensuring that your images are responsive is essential. Responsive images automatically adjust to fit different screen sizes and resolutions, providing an optimal viewing experience across devices. Use HTML5's `srcset` attribute to define different image sources for various screen sizes, allowing browsers to select the most appropriate image based on the user's device. This practice not only improves user experience but also enhances page load times and SEO.

Implementing structured data for images can further enhance their visibility in search results. Structured data, also known as schema markup, provides search engines with additional information about your images, such as their subject, creator, and license. By adding image-related structured data to your HTML, you can improve the chances of your images appearing in rich snippets and other enhanced search results. This can increase click-through rates and drive more traffic to your site. Use Google's Structured Data Markup Helper or schema.org to add structured data to your images.

Leveraging browser caching for images can improve page load times and user experience. Caching stores copies of your images on users' devices, allowing them to load faster on subsequent visits. Use caching headers to specify how long images should be stored in the browser cache. This reduces the need for repeated downloads, speeds up page load times, and enhances SEO. Configure caching settings in your website's server or use a content delivery network (CDN) to manage image caching efficiently.

Regularly updating and auditing your image content is crucial for maintaining optimal performance and SEO. Conduct periodic audits to identify outdated, low-quality, or irrelevant images and replace them with fresh, high-quality alternatives. Ensure that all new images are optimised according to the best practices outlined above. Regular updates not only keep your content relevant and engaging but also signal to search engines that your site is actively maintained, which can positively impact your rankings.

By implementing these comprehensive strategies for optimising image content, you can enhance the visual appeal, user engagement, and SEO performance of your website. Properly optimised images contribute to faster page load times, improved accessibility, higher search rankings, and a better overall user experience. Embrace these best practices to ensure your images are effectively supporting your digital marketing efforts and driving meaningful results.

Optimising Voice Content

Voice search is rapidly transforming the landscape of digital interactions, reshaping how users interact with search engines and access information. With the proliferation of voice-activated devices like smart speakers, virtual assistants, and mobile voice search, optimising for voice search has become an essential component of modern SEO strategies. This section delves into the nuances of optimising voice content, exploring the distinct strategies required to effectively cater to this growing trend.

One of the fundamental differences between voice search and traditional text-based search lies in the nature of the queries. Voice searches are typically longer, more conversational, and often posed in the form of complete questions or phrases. As a result, optimising for voice search requires a shift from focusing on short, concise keywords to embracing natural language keywords and phrases that mimic how people speak.

For instance, while a text-based search might be "best Italian restaurant," a voice search is more likely to be "What is the best Italian restaurant near me?" To effectively optimise for voice search, it is crucial to identify and incorporate these natural language queries into your content. This involves conducting thorough keyword research to understand the questions and phrases your target audience is likely to use when speaking rather than typing.

Leveraging tools like Google's Keyword Planner, AnswerThePublic, and SEMrush can help identify common conversational queries. Once these keywords and phrases are identified, seamlessly integrate them into your content, including headings, subheadings, and body text. This approach ensures that your content aligns with the way users naturally speak, increasing the likelihood of your site appearing in voice search results.

Featured snippets, as discussed in a previous chapter, and often referred to as "position zero," play a pivotal role in voice search optimisation. These are concise, direct answers to user queries that appear at the top of Google's search results. Given their prominence, featured snippets are frequently used by voice-activated devices to provide spoken responses to user questions. Therefore, securing a featured snippet position can significantly enhance your visibility in voice search results.

To optimise your content for featured snippets, focus on providing clear, concise, and well-structured answers to common questions related to your industry. Use headings and bullet points to break down information into easily digestible segments. Additionally, include direct answers to questions within the first few sentences of your content, as search engines often pull snippets from the initial paragraphs.

Creating comprehensive FAQ pages that address common queries in your niche can also improve your chances of capturing featured snippets. Ensure that your answers are informative, accurate, and directly address the user's intent. By positioning your content to provide immediate value, you increase the likelihood of it being selected as a featured snippet and subsequently used in voice search responses.

Local SEO optimisation is crucial for voice search, as a significant proportion of voice queries are location-based. Users frequently rely on voice search to find local businesses, services, and information, making it essential for your business information to be accurate, consistent, and easily accessible across all online platforms.

Start by claiming and optimising your Google Business Profile listing. Ensure that all details, including your business name, address, phone number, and hours of operation, are accurate and up to date. Encourage customers to leave reviews, as positive feedback can enhance your local search rankings and increase the likelihood of your business being recommended in voice searches.

Additionally, incorporate location-based keywords into your content. For example, if you run a bakery in Dublin City, include phrases like "best bakery in Dublin City" or "top-rated bakery near Dublin 2" in your content. This approach helps search engines associate your business with specific locations, improving your chances of appearing in local voice search results.

Creating locally-focused content, such as blog posts about community events, local news, or area-specific tips, can further enhance your local SEO efforts. This content not only engages your audience but also signals to search engines that your site is relevant to local users, boosting your visibility in location-based voice searches.

Structured data and schema markup play a vital role in optimising for voice search. By adding structured data to your website, you provide search engines with additional context about your content, making it easier for them to understand and categorise your information. This, in turn, enhances your chances of appearing in voice search results.

Implement schema markup for various elements of your site, such as articles, products, events, and local business information. For voice search, focus on marking up content that addresses common questions, provides detailed business information, and highlights important data points. Use Google's Structured Data Markup Helper or Schema.org to guide your implementation of schema markup.

Structured data can also improve your chances of being featured in rich snippets, which are frequently used in voice search responses. By providing search engines with well-structured information, you increase the likelihood of your content being selected as the best answer to user queries.

Voice searches are often conducted on mobile devices, making mobile optimisation a critical component of voice search SEO. Ensure that your website is fully optimised for mobile, with a responsive design that adapts seamlessly to different screen sizes. Fast loading times, easy navigation, and a user-friendly interface are essential for providing a positive mobile experience.

Google's mobile-first indexing means that the mobile version of your site is considered the primary version for ranking purposes. This shift underscores the importance of optimising your mobile site for both traditional and voice search. Regularly test your site's mobile performance using tools like Google's Mobile-Friendly Test and PageSpeed Insights to identify and address any issues.

To optimise for voice search, your content must be conversational and user-focused. Write in a natural, engaging tone that reflects how people speak. Use simple language, avoid jargon, and aim for clarity and conciseness. Address the user's intent directly and provide valuable, actionable information.

Incorporate long-tail keywords and question-based phrases into your content to align with the nature of voice queries. For example, instead of focusing solely on the keyword "SEO tips," include variations like "What are the best SEO tips for small businesses?" or "How can I improve my SEO rankings quickly?"

Creating conversational content not only improves your chances of appearing in voice search results but also enhances the overall user experience, making your site more engaging and accessible to a broader audience.

Search engines prioritise content that provides a positive user experience. Factors such as dwell time, bounce rate, and user engagement are taken into account when ranking content for voice search. To optimise for these factors, focus on creating high-quality, engaging content that encourages users to spend more time on your site.

Incorporate multimedia elements like videos, images, and interactive content to enhance the user experience. Use clear headings, subheadings, and bullet points to break up text and improve readability. Encourage user interaction through comments, social sharing, and calls to action.

Regularly update your content to keep it fresh and relevant. Voice search users often seek the most up-to-date information, so maintaining current and accurate content can improve your chances of ranking well in voice search results.

Continuously monitor and analyse your voice search performance to refine your optimisation strategies. Use tools like Google Analytics and Google Search Console to track metrics such as voice search traffic, keyword performance, and user behaviour. Identify trends and patterns to understand how users are interacting with your voice-optimised content.

Set up alerts and notifications to stay informed about changes in voice search trends and algorithm updates. Regularly review and adjust your voice search strategy based on data-driven insights to ensure ongoing improvement and success.

By implementing these comprehensive strategies for optimising voice content, you can enhance your visibility, engagement, and SEO performance in the rapidly evolving landscape of voice search. Embrace the unique challenges and opportunities of voice search optimisation to stay ahead of the competition and connect with your audience in meaningful ways.

Leveraging Diverse Content Formats for Enhanced SEO

Incorporating a mix of content formats into your digital strategy can significantly boost your SEO efforts. Each format has its unique strengths and can engage different segments of your audience. By optimising videos, images, text, and voice content, you create a comprehensive and engaging user experience that appeals to both search engines and users.

An integrated content strategy that combines different formats can maximise your reach and impact. For example, a blog post can be accompanied by an engaging video, relevant images, and a downloadable podcast episode. This approach caters to various user preferences and enhances the overall value of your content. Videos can explain complex topics more clearly, images can break up text and make content more visually appealing, and voice content like podcasts can reach users on the go.

Regularly monitor the performance of your multimedia content using analytics tools. Track metrics such as views, engagement, click-through rates, and conversions. Use these insights to refine your content strategy and ensure continuous improvement. For instance, if a particular type of video content generates high engagement, consider producing more of that style. Conversely, if certain images are not performing well, analyse why and adjust your approach accordingly.

The digital landscape is constantly evolving, and staying updated with the latest trends and best practices is crucial. Attend industry conferences, participate in webinars, and follow reputable SEO blogs to keep your knowledge current. This proactive approach ensures that your strategies remain effective and competitive. Trends such as augmented reality (AR) in marketing, the rise of short-form videos on platforms like TikTok, and the increasing use of voice assistants like Alexa and Siri are all areas where staying informed can give you an edge.

High-quality, engaging multimedia content not only enhances user experience but also improves your site's visibility and ranking in search results. Search engines increasingly prioritise content that provides value and engagement, and diverse content formats help meet these criteria. For instance, Google's algorithms favour pages that keep users engaged, and multimedia content can significantly lower bounce rates and increase the time users spend on your site.

By embracing videos, images, text, and voice content, and ensuring each format is meticulously optimised, you can create a robust, effective digital strategy that meets the needs of your audience and achieves your business goals. This means not only creating content that is visually and audibly appealing but also ensuring that it is accessible, fast-loading, and optimised for search engines. Use structured data to help search engines understand and present your content better in search results, and always consider user intent when creating content.

Moreover, consider the cross-promotion of content across various platforms to enhance visibility and engagement. For example, promote your videos and podcasts on social media, embed them in relevant blog posts, and include transcripts for better accessibility and SEO. Cross-promotion ensures that your content reaches a broader audience and maximises its impact.

A multifaceted approach to content creation and optimisation is key to a successful digital strategy. By understanding and leveraging the strengths of different content formats, continuously monitoring performance, staying updated with industry trends, and ensuring that every piece of content is optimised for SEO, you can create an engaging, high-performing digital presence. This holistic approach not only improves your SEO rankings but also enhances user satisfaction and drives business growth.

CHAPTER 12
CONTENT DISTRIBUTION AND PROMOTION

Creating high-quality content is only half the battle. The real challenge lies in ensuring that your content reaches the right audience. Content distribution and promotion are crucial aspects of any successful content strategy. This chapter delves into the importance of content distribution and promotion, covering various strategies for disseminating content, the role of social media in SEO, and the effectiveness of email marketing and other distribution channels.

Effective content dissemination requires a strategic approach to ensure that your content is not only seen but also engaged with by your target audience. Leveraging owned media channels such as your website, blog, and email newsletters is a fundamental starting point. These platforms allow you to maintain control over your content and ensure that it reaches your audience in the way you intend. Regularly updating your blog with fresh, relevant content and using email newsletters to inform your subscribers about new posts and updates can significantly enhance your content reach.

Owned media gives you a direct line to your audience, allowing you to cultivate a loyal following. However, it's essential to ensure that your content is optimised for these channels. This includes using compelling headlines, engaging visuals, and clear calls to action to drive engagement and conversions.

Earned media plays a crucial role in content dissemination. This involves gaining exposure through third-party platforms and influencers who share your content with their audiences. Public relations efforts, guest blogging, influencer partnerships, and getting your content featured in industry publications are effective ways to achieve this. Earned media helps build credibility and trust, as endorsements from respected sources can enhance your content's perceived value. By collaborating with influencers and industry leaders, you can tap into their established audiences and expand your reach.

Paid media is another vital component of a robust content distribution strategy. This includes paid advertising on search engines, social media platforms, and other websites. Using tools like Google Ads, Facebook Ads, and sponsored content on relevant websites can increase your content's visibility and drive targeted traffic to your site. While this approach requires a financial investment, it can yield significant returns by placing your content in front of a broader, yet targeted audience. It's important to carefully plan and monitor your paid campaigns to ensure you get the best return on investment.

Content syndication is a powerful strategy to extend the reach of your content. By republishing your content on third-party websites, you can tap into new audiences who may not have found your content otherwise. Syndication partnerships with industry-related websites, online magazines, and blogs can drive more traffic to your site and increase your content's visibility. However, it's crucial to select reputable syndication partners to maintain the quality and credibility of your content.

SEO is fundamental to content dissemination. Optimising your content with relevant keywords, meta descriptions, and tags ensures that it appears in search engine results, making it easier for users to find your content organically. Consistently high-quality content that adheres to SEO best practices will gradually improve your search rankings and drive more organic traffic to your site. This involves not only optimising your current content but also performing regular SEO audits to ensure ongoing performance.

Influencer marketing is another effective strategy for content dissemination. By collaborating with influencers who have a substantial following in your industry, you can leverage their reach to promote your content. Influencers can share your content with their audience, write guest posts, or create joint content projects that highlight your brand. This strategy not only enhances your content's visibility but also builds credibility through association with respected figures in your industry.

Content partnerships and collaborations can also play a significant role in content dissemination. Partnering with other brands or content creators to co-create content can help you reach new audiences. This could involve joint webinars, co-authored articles, or collaborative videos. Such partnerships can expand your reach and provide valuable cross-promotion opportunities.

Social media platforms are indispensable tools for content promotion and play a significant role in SEO. When you share content on social media, you increase its visibility and the chances of it being shared by others, thereby expanding its reach. Social media engagement, such as likes, shares, and comments, can drive traffic to your website, signal to search engines that your content is valuable, and improve your rankings.

Each social media platform has unique features that can be leveraged to maximise content reach. For instance, Facebook's robust ad platform allows for highly targeted advertising campaigns, while Twitter's real-time engagement capabilities can drive instant traffic to your content. LinkedIn is particularly effective for B2B content, providing a platform for professional engagement and networking. Instagram and Pinterest, with their visual focus, are ideal for promoting image and video content.

Creating shareable content tailored for each platform can significantly boost engagement. For example, infographics, short videos, and engaging images tend to perform well on visual platforms like Instagram and Pinterest. Meanwhile, in-depth articles and industry insights may be better suited for LinkedIn. By understanding the strengths of each platform, you can tailor your content to maximise engagement and drive traffic to your site.

Utilising social media analytics tools can help you understand which types of content resonate most with your audience on each platform. Tools like Facebook Insights, Twitter Analytics, and LinkedIn Analytics provide valuable data on engagement rates, audience demographics, and optimal posting times. This information can guide your content strategy and help you refine your approach to maximise reach and impact.

Paid social media campaigns can also be highly effective for promoting content. Platforms like Facebook and Instagram offer advanced targeting options that allow you to reach specific demographics, interests, and behaviours. By investing in paid campaigns, you can amplify your content's reach and drive more traffic to your site.

Engaging with your audience on social media is crucial for building relationships and fostering loyalty. Respond to comments, participate in discussions, and share user-generated content to create a sense of community around your brand. This engagement not only enhances your content's visibility but also builds trust and credibility with your audience.

Leveraging social media influencers to promote your content can also yield significant benefits. Influencers can share your content with their followers, write reviews, or create sponsored posts that highlight your brand. By collaborating with influencers who align with your brand values and have a substantial following, you can reach new audiences and boost your content's visibility.

Email marketing remains one of the most effective channels for content distribution. With a well-maintained email list, you can directly reach your audience and share new content, updates, and promotional materials. Personalised email campaigns that cater to the interests and behaviours of your subscribers can significantly increase engagement rates. Regular newsletters, exclusive content offers, and automated email sequences ensure that your audience remains engaged and informed about your latest content.

Segmenting your email list based on subscriber preferences, behaviour, and demographics can help you deliver more relevant content. For example, you can create segments for different types of content, such as blog posts, product updates, or industry news. By tailoring your email campaigns to each segment, you can increase open rates, click-through rates, and overall engagement.

Incorporating multimedia elements into your email campaigns can also enhance engagement. Videos, infographics, and interactive content can make your emails more engaging and encourage subscribers to click through to your website. Additionally, using compelling subject lines and personalised greetings can increase the likelihood of your emails being opened and read.

Other distribution channels should not be overlooked. RSS feeds, for example, allow users to subscribe to your content and receive updates automatically. This can be particularly effective for maintaining engagement with a dedicated audience. Additionally, forums and online communities related to your industry can be valuable platforms for sharing your content and engaging with potential customers. By participating in discussions and providing valuable insights, you can establish yourself as an authority in your field and drive traffic to your content.

Podcasting is another emerging channel for content distribution. Creating a podcast allows you to reach audiences who prefer audio content and can be a powerful way to share your expertise and insights. Promoting your podcast episodes through your existing channels and encouraging listeners to subscribe and leave reviews can expand your reach and engagement.

Webinars and online events are also effective content distribution channels. Hosting webinars on topics relevant to your audience can position you as an industry expert and provide valuable content that can be repurposed into blog posts, videos, and social media updates. Promoting your webinars through email marketing, social media, and your website can drive registrations and engagement.

Guest posting on reputable websites and blogs in your industry can help you reach new audiences and drive traffic to your site. By contributing valuable content to other platforms, you can establish yourself as a thought leader and attract new followers to your brand. Ensure that your guest posts include links back to your website to drive referral traffic.

An integrated content strategy that combines different formats can maximise your reach and impact. For example, a blog post can be accompanied by an engaging video, relevant images, and a downloadable podcast episode. This approach caters to various user preferences and enhances the overall value of your content. By leveraging multiple content formats, you can engage a wider audience and provide a richer, more comprehensive user experience.

Integrating your content strategy across various channels ensures a cohesive brand message and consistent user experience. For instance, promoting a new product launch through a combination of blog posts, social media updates, email newsletters, and video content can create a unified campaign that reaches your audience through multiple touchpoints.

Regularly monitor the performance of your multimedia content using analytics tools. Track metrics such as views, engagement, click-through rates, and conversions. Use these insights to refine your content strategy and ensure continuous improvement. By analysing the data, you can identify what works and what doesn't, allowing you to adjust your approach and optimise your content distribution efforts.

Tools like Google Analytics, social media analytics platforms, and email marketing software provide valuable data on content performance. By regularly reviewing these metrics, you can gain insights into audience behaviour, preferences, and engagement patterns. Use this information to make data-driven decisions and optimise your content strategy for better results.

The digital landscape is constantly evolving, and staying updated with the latest trends and best practices is crucial. Attend industry conferences, participate in webinars, and follow reputable SEO and digital marketing blogs to keep your knowledge current. Engaging with thought leaders and experts in your field can provide valuable insights and help you stay ahead of the curve. As new technologies and platforms emerge, it's essential to adapt your content distribution strategy accordingly. For example, the rise of new social media platforms or changes in search engine algorithms can impact how your content is discovered and consumed. Staying informed about these developments ensures that your strategy remains relevant and effective.

Engage with Your Audience

Content distribution is not just about pushing your content out to as many channels as possible; it's also about engaging with your audience and building relationships. Responding to comments on your blog, social media posts, and videos can foster a sense of community and loyalty among your audience. Encouraging user-generated content, such as reviews, testimonials, and social media shares, can also enhance your content's reach and credibility.

By actively engaging with your audience, you can gather feedback and insights that can inform your content strategy. Understanding what resonates with your audience and addressing their needs and preferences can help you create more targeted and effective content.

User-generated content (UGC) is a powerful tool for content distribution and promotion. Encouraging your audience to create and share content related to your brand can amplify your reach and build trust. UGC includes reviews, testimonials, social media posts, and videos created by your customers. Sharing this content on your channels not only boosts your credibility but also fosters a sense of community and engagement.

To leverage UGC effectively, create campaigns that encourage your audience to share their experiences with your products or services. Offer incentives, such as contests or discounts, to motivate participation. Highlighting UGC on your website, social media, and email newsletters can also inspire others to contribute and engage with your brand.

Create Shareable Content

Creating content that is easily shareable is essential for maximising your reach. Content that resonates with your audience and is visually appealing is more likely to be shared on social media and other platforms. Infographics, memes, videos, and interactive content are particularly effective at capturing attention and encouraging shares.

To create shareable content, focus on storytelling and emotional appeal. Content that evokes strong emotions, such as humour, inspiration, or empathy, is more likely to be shared. Additionally, incorporating trending topics and current events into your content can increase its relevance and shareability.

Collaborating with Influencers

Collaborating with influencers can significantly boost your content distribution efforts. Influencers have established audiences that trust their recommendations and insights. By partnering with influencers who align with your brand values and target audience, you can expand your reach and enhance your credibility.

Influencer collaborations can take various forms, including sponsored posts, product reviews, guest blog posts, and social media takeovers. When selecting influencers to collaborate with, consider their audience demographics, engagement rates, and content style. Working with influencers who have a genuine connection to your brand can lead to more authentic and impactful content.

Maximising Reach Through Paid Promotion

While organic reach is essential, paid promotion can amplify your content distribution efforts. Investing in paid advertising on search engines, social media platforms, and other websites can increase your content's visibility and drive targeted traffic to your site.

Platforms like Google Ads and Facebook Ads offer advanced targeting options that allow you to reach specific demographics, interests, and behaviours. By carefully planning and monitoring your paid campaigns, you can ensure a positive return on investment and maximise your content's reach and impact.

The Power of Storytelling

At the heart of successful content distribution is compelling storytelling. Stories have the power to captivate, engage, and inspire your audience. By weaving narratives into your content, you can create a deeper connection with your audience and make your content more memorable.

Effective storytelling involves understanding your audience's needs, values, and aspirations. Crafting narratives that resonate with these elements can evoke strong emotions and drive engagement. Whether through blog posts, videos, social media updates, or podcasts, storytelling can elevate your content and make it more shareable.

Success

Content distribution and promotion are critical to success. By leveraging a variety of content formats and optimising them for SEO, you can create a robust, effective digital strategy that meets the needs of your audience and achieves your business goals. Whether through owned, earned, or paid media, integrating your content strategy across multiple channels ensures a cohesive and impactful approach.

Engaging with your audience, leveraging user-generated content, creating shareable content, collaborating with influencers, and maximising reach through paid promotion are all essential elements of a successful content distribution strategy. By staying updated with trends and continuously refining your approach based on data and insights, you can ensure that your content reaches its full potential and drives sustainable business growth.

CHAPTER 13
OFF-PAGE SEO AND LOCAL STRATEGIES

In the expansive world of SEO, optimising your website's content and structure is only part of the equation. Off-page SEO plays a crucial role in determining your site's authority, relevance, and overall ranking in search engine results. This chapter delves into the critical components of off-page SEO, including link building, social media integration, and local SEO strategies, providing you with the tools and knowledge to enhance your digital presence effectively.

Link Building

Backlinks, or inbound links, are links from one website to another. They are a fundamental component of off-page SEO and are often seen as votes of confidence from one site to another. The importance of backlinks cannot be overstated for several reasons.

Backlinks are critical for search engine ranking because they are a primary factor that search engines like Google use to determine a site's authority and relevance. A site with numerous high-quality backlinks from reputable sources is more likely to be seen as trustworthy and authoritative, leading to higher rankings in search results.

Backlinks drive referral traffic. When a user clicks on a link on another site that directs them to your website, this is known as referral traffic. High-quality backlinks can lead to increased traffic from users who are already interested in topics related to your content.

Backlinks help with faster indexing. Search engine bots follow links from one page to another, which means backlinks can help search engines discover and index your pages more quickly.

Acquiring High-Quality Links

Acquiring high-quality backlinks requires a strategic approach. Here are some effective techniques to build a robust backlink profile…

Creating high-quality, valuable content that others naturally want to link to is the cornerstone of any successful link-building strategy. This includes blog posts, infographics, videos, and research reports. Content that provides value, whether through in-depth analysis, unique insights, or engaging visuals, is more likely to attract backlinks.

Guest blogging involves writing articles for other reputable websites in your industry. This not only helps you reach a broader audience but also provides an opportunity to include backlinks to your own site. When guest blogging, focus on high-quality sites with a good reputation.

Engaging in broken link building involves finding broken links on other websites and offering your content as a replacement. Tools like Ahrefs and Check My Links can help identify broken links on relevant sites. Once found, you can reach out to the site owner, informing them of the broken link and suggesting your content as a replacement.

Collaborating with influencers and industry experts can also lead to valuable backlinks. These individuals often have established audiences and websites with high domain authority. Building relationships through social media, industry events, and direct outreach can result in backlinks from their platforms.

Creating shareable assets such as infographics, videos, and interactive content can also drive backlinks. These types of content are often more engaging and can be easily shared across different platforms, increasing the likelihood of acquiring backlinks.

PR and Link Building

The influence of both digital and traditional public relations (PR) on link building is significant and multifaceted. Link building, a core component of SEO, involves acquiring hyperlinks from other websites to your own, which signals to search engines that your site is a credible and valuable resource. Effective PR strategies, whether digital or traditional, can be powerful tools in securing these high-quality backlinks, thereby enhancing your site's authority, visibility, and rankings.

Digital PR has become a cornerstone of modern link-building strategies. It involves creating and promoting content online with the goal of attracting media coverage and backlinks from authoritative websites. Digital PR is particularly effective because it merges the principles of traditional public relations with the dynamics of digital marketing, leveraging the internet's vast reach to amplify brand visibility.

One of the key strategies in digital PR for link building is content creation and outreach. This involves crafting compelling stories, press releases, blog posts, infographics, or videos that are newsworthy or highly informative. Once created, this content is distributed to journalists, bloggers, and influencers who might find it valuable for their audiences. When these figures share your content or reference it in their own articles, they often include a link back to your website, providing a valuable backlink.

Another effective digital PR tactic is engaging with online communities and forums. By participating in discussions on platforms like Reddit, Quora, or industry-specific forums, you can share insights, provide value, and subtly promote your content. This approach can lead to organic backlinks as users in these communities link back to your site when they find your content useful or relevant to ongoing discussions.

Digital PR also leverages social media as a tool for link building. When content is shared on platforms like Twitter, LinkedIn, or Facebook, it has the potential to be picked up by others, including bloggers and journalists, who might link to it from their own sites. Social shares do not directly impact SEO rankings, but they can drive traffic to your content, increase its visibility, and indirectly lead to more backlinks.

Traditional PR, while often perceived as separate from digital strategies, also plays a crucial role in link building. Traditional PR focuses on building relationships with media outlets, journalists, and influencers to gain coverage in newspapers, magazines, television, and radio. Although these media do not typically provide direct links to websites, the coverage they generate can significantly influence digital link-building efforts.

For instance, a feature in a reputable newspaper or magazine can increase your brand's credibility and visibility, prompting bloggers, industry experts, and other online content creators to mention your brand in their digital content. These mentions often come with backlinks, as these digital platforms reference the traditional media coverage as part of their narrative.

Moreover, press releases distributed through traditional PR channels can be picked up by digital news outlets, which are more likely to include hyperlinks to your website. The key is to ensure that press releases are optimised for digital platforms, including a clear, accessible link to your website within the content.

Another way traditional PR influences link building is through event management. Hosting or sponsoring events, conferences, or seminars can attract media coverage and social media buzz, leading to mentions and links from websites that cover the event or discuss its outcomes. These events often generate newsworthy content that is picked up by both traditional and digital media, creating a ripple effect of backlinks to your site.

The most effective link-building strategies often involve a combination of both digital and traditional PR efforts. Traditional PR can establish your brand's authority and trustworthiness, which digital PR can then amplify by securing online media coverage and backlinks. This synergy ensures a comprehensive approach to link building, leveraging the strengths of both methods.

For example, a traditional PR campaign might secure an interview for your CEO in a major print publication. Following this, a digital PR strategy could promote the interview online, distribute it across social media channels, and pitch it to bloggers and digital journalists who might link back to your site when discussing the interview's insights.

Moreover, traditional PR efforts can lay the groundwork for successful digital PR campaigns. Establishing strong relationships with journalists and influencers through traditional methods can make it easier to pitch digital content to them later, ensuring that your digital PR campaigns are well-received and more likely to result in valuable backlinks.

In essence, the integration of digital and traditional PR in link-building strategies provides a robust and multifaceted approach to increasing your website's authority and search engine rankings. While digital PR excels in directly acquiring backlinks through online content and outreach, traditional PR supports these efforts by building brand credibility and generating media coverage that can lead to organic link building. Together, they form a powerful combination that enhances the effectiveness of your overall SEO strategy.

Influence of Social Signals or Links on SEO

Social signals refer to the engagement your content receives on social media platforms, including likes, shares, comments, and overall interactions. While there has been debate over how directly social signals impact SEO, their influence on your site's visibility and traffic is undeniable. Social signals can lead to increased traffic, which indirectly affects your SEO. When content is widely shared and engaged with on social media, it can drive significant traffic to your website. This increase in traffic can lead to higher engagement metrics, such as longer time on site and lower bounce rates, which search engines consider when ranking pages.

Social signals can enhance brand visibility and recognition. A strong social media presence can increase your brand's visibility, making it more likely that users will search for your brand directly. Branded searches are a positive signal to search engines, indicating that your brand is reputable and relevant. Social media platforms themselves are search engines. Platforms like YouTube, TikTok, Facebook and X have their own search functions that can drive traffic to your content.

Optimising your content for these platforms can increase your visibility within these ecosystems.

Developing a comprehensive social media strategy is essential for leveraging the power of social signals. Here are some strategies to enhance your social media presence.

Creating and sharing high-quality content that resonates with your audience is the foundation of an effective social media strategy. This includes blog posts, videos, infographics, and interactive content. Tailor your content to the preferences of your audience on each platform.

Engaging with your audience by responding to comments, participating in discussions, and sharing user-generated content can foster a sense of community and loyalty. Active engagement not only boosts your social signals but also strengthens your relationship with your audience.

As previously mentioned, utilising social media advertising can amplify your reach and drive targeted traffic to your site. Platforms like Facebook, Instagram, and LinkedIn offer advanced targeting options that allow you to reach specific demographics and interests.

Collaborating with influencers and brand advocates can expand your reach and enhance your credibility. Influencers have established audiences that trust their recommendations. Partnering with influencers who align with your brand values can lead to increased visibility and engagement.

Regularly analysing your social media performance using analytics tools can provide insights into what content resonates with your audience and how your social signals are impacting your SEO. Use these insights to refine your social media strategy continuously.

Local SEO

Local SEO is crucial for small businesses that rely on local customers. Optimising for local search can increase your visibility to potential customers in your geographic area, driving traffic, leads, and sales. Local SEO helps businesses appear in local search results and map listings, which are prominently displayed in search engine results pages (SERPs). This increased visibility can drive foot traffic to your physical location and generate local leads.

Local SEO builds trust and credibility within your community. When your business appears in local search results and has positive reviews, it enhances your reputation and encourages local customers to choose your services. Local SEO can give small businesses a competitive edge. By optimising your online presence for local search, you can compete more effectively with larger, national brands that may not be targeting your specific geographic area.

Claiming and optimising your Google Business Profile (formerly Google My Business) is a critical component of local SEO. A well-optimised GBP listing can significantly enhance your visibility in local search results and attract local customers. Ensure your GBP listing is complete and accurate, including your business name, address, phone number, website, and business hours. Add high-quality images of your business, products, and services to make your listing more engaging. Regularly update your GBP listing with posts about promotions, events, and news. This keeps your listing fresh and provides additional information to potential customers.

Encourage customers to leave reviews on your GBP listing. Positive reviews can improve your visibility and credibility in local search results. Respond to reviews, both positive and negative, to show that you value customer feedback and are committed to providing excellent service. Reviews play a significant role in local SEO and can influence potential customers' decisions. Encouraging and managing reviews is essential for building trust and improving your local search rankings. Encourage satisfied customers to leave reviews by providing excellent service and asking for feedback. Make it easy for customers to leave reviews by providing links to your review profiles on your website, in emails, and on receipts. Responding to reviews shows that you value customer feedback and are committed to improving your services. Thank customers for positive reviews and address any issues raised in negative reviews professionally and constructively.

Engaging with your local community through social media, local events, and partnerships can also boost your local SEO. Building strong relationships within your community enhances your reputation and encourages local customers to support your business.

By focusing on link building, social media integration, and local SEO strategies, you can enhance your off-page SEO efforts and drive significant traffic and engagement to your website. These strategies are essential for building authority, credibility, and visibility in the competitive digital landscape. Continuously refining your approach and staying updated with the latest trends and best practices will ensure long-term success and growth for your business.

CHAPTER 14
SEO TOOLS & ANALYTICS

In the (sometimes annoyingly) dynamic world of SEO, staying ahead of the curve requires not only a solid understanding of foundational practices but also an awareness of the latest tools, techniques, and trends. This chapter delves into the essential SEO tools that can enhance your strategies, the importance of robust analytics and reporting, and emerging practices that are shaping the future of SEO. By leveraging these tools and insights, you can refine your approach, maximise your impact, and stay competitive in an ever-evolving digital landscape.

SEO Tools

In the realm of SEO, having the right tools at your disposal can make a significant difference in your ability to analyse, optimise, and monitor your website's performance. Here, we explore some essential tools that every SEO professional should be familiar with, as well as the benefits of custom tools and APIs.

Ahrefs: Known for its comprehensive backlink analysis capabilities, Ahrefs is a powerful tool for SEO professionals. It offers a robust suite of features, including keyword research, site audits, competitor analysis, and content exploration. Ahrefs' ability to track backlinks and analyse the link profile of any website makes it invaluable for developing effective link-building strategies.

SEMrush: SEMrush is an all-in-one SEO tool that provides insights into keyword rankings, site audits, competitor analysis, and advertising research. Its keyword research capabilities are particularly strong, allowing users to discover long-tail keywords and understand the competitive landscape. SEMrush also offers tools for tracking organic traffic, monitoring social media performance, and identifying backlink opportunities.

Moz: Moz offers a range of SEO tools designed to help with keyword research, link building, site audits, and rank tracking. Moz's Domain Authority (DA) metric is widely used in the industry to gauge the quality of a website. Moz also provides a Chrome extension, MozBar, which allows users to quickly assess SEO metrics while browsing the web.

These tools provide critical insights and data that can help you understand your site's performance, identify opportunities for improvement, and develop strategies to enhance your SEO efforts.

While commercial SEO tools like Ahrefs, SEMrush, and Moz offer a wide array of features, there are times when custom tools and APIs can provide additional value. Custom tools can be tailored to meet the specific needs of your business or industry, allowing for more precise data analysis and reporting.

Custom Tools: Developing custom SEO tools can help you address unique challenges and optimise specific aspects of your website. For example, a custom tool might be designed to track local SEO performance, analyse content quality, or monitor technical SEO issues. By focusing on your specific requirements, custom tools can provide deeper insights and more actionable data.

APIs: Many SEO tools offer APIs that allow you to integrate their data and functionality into your own systems. By leveraging APIs, you can automate data collection, streamline reporting, and integrate SEO insights with other business intelligence tools. This can enhance your ability to make data-driven decisions and optimise your SEO strategy in real-time.

Analytics and Reporting

Accurate and comprehensive analytics are the backbone of effective SEO. Understanding how to set up and interpret analytics data is essential for refining your strategies and achieving your SEO goals. In this section, we explore the importance of analytics and provide detailed guidance on setting up and using Google Analytics, interpreting data, and employing advanced tracking techniques.

Google Analytics is a powerful tool that provides a wealth of information about your website's performance. Proper setup is crucial for capturing accurate data and gaining meaningful insights.

Account Creation: Start by creating a Google Analytics account and setting up a property for your website. This involves adding a tracking code to your site's HTML, which allows Google Analytics to collect data on user interactions.

Goals and Conversions: Define specific goals within Google Analytics to track important actions on your site, such as form submissions, product purchases, or newsletter sign-ups. Setting up conversion tracking helps you understand how well your site is achieving its objectives.

Custom Dashboards: Create custom dashboards to visualise key metrics and track performance over time. Custom dashboards can be tailored to display the most relevant data for your business, making it easier to monitor progress and identify trends.

Collecting data is only the first step; the real value lies in interpreting this data to inform and refine your SEO strategies.

Traffic Sources: Analyse the sources of your website traffic to understand where your visitors are coming from. This includes organic search, direct traffic, referral traffic, and social media. Understanding traffic sources helps you identify which channels are most effective and where to focus your efforts.

User Behaviour: Examine user behaviour metrics such as bounce rate, average session duration, and pages per session. These metrics provide insights into how users interact with your site and can highlight areas for improvement in user experience and content engagement.

Conversion Analysis: Assess conversion rates for different goals and identify any barriers to conversion. Analysing conversion paths can reveal opportunities to streamline the user journey and increase conversion rates.

For more in-depth insights, advanced tracking techniques can be employed to capture additional data and provide a more comprehensive view of your website's performance.

Event Tracking: Use event tracking to monitor specific user interactions, such as clicks on buttons, downloads, and video plays. Event tracking provides granular data on user behaviour that goes beyond standard page views.

Enhanced Ecommerce: For ecommerce websites, setting up enhanced ecommerce tracking in Google Analytics allows you to capture detailed data on product performance, sales funnels, and customer behaviour. This information is invaluable for optimising your online store and increasing sales.

Custom Dimensions and Metrics: Implement custom dimensions and metrics to track data that is specific to your business. This might include tracking user segments, content types, or custom interactions that are not covered by default Google Analytics reports.

CHAPTER 15

EMERGING SEO PRACTICES

The SEO landscape is constantly evolving, with new technologies and trends shaping the way we approach optimisation. Staying ahead of these changes is crucial for maintaining a competitive edge. In this section, we explore emerging SEO practices, including the impact of AI and machine learning, voice search optimisation, SEO for connected devices and IoT, and SEO for AR and VR.

AI and Machine Learning Impacts

Artificial Intelligence (AI) and machine learning are revolutionising SEO by enabling more sophisticated data analysis, personalisation, and predictive capabilities.

Content Optimisation: AI-powered tools can analyse large datasets to identify content opportunities, optimise for user intent, and predict future trends. Machine learning algorithms can also personalise content recommendations based on user behaviour and preferences.

Search Algorithms: Search engines like Google use machine learning to improve their algorithms and deliver more relevant search results. Understanding how these algorithms work and how they prioritise content can help you adapt your SEO strategies accordingly.

Automation: AI can automate repetitive SEO tasks, such as keyword research, site audits, and performance monitoring. This allows SEO professionals to focus on higher-level strategy and creative efforts.

As digital innovation continues to accelerate, Google remains at the forefront of integrating advanced artificial intelligence (AI) into its search engine to enhance user experiences, improve the quality of search results, and facilitate the discovery of relevant information. The latest leap forward in this technological journey is the introduction of cutting-edge generative AI technology aimed at transforming how we interact with search engines. This new development, aptly named Search Generative Experience (SGE), represents a significant evolution in the way Google handles search queries, promising to redefine the search landscape.

For years, Google has been pushing the boundaries of what search engines can do, introducing groundbreaking technologies like Bidirectional Encoder Representations from Transformers (BERT) and the Multitask Unified Model (MUM). These innovations have revolutionised how search engines understand and process natural language, enabling them to deliver more accurate and contextually relevant search results. However, the advent of SGE marks a new frontier in search technology, where generative AI takes centre stage to create a more interactive, intuitive, and engaging search experience.

Generative AI, at its core, is a form of artificial intelligence capable of creating new content—whether that be text, images, videos, or even music—based on existing data. It doesn't merely replicate information; it synthesises it in new ways, offering fresh perspectives and insights that go beyond simple keyword matching or basic data retrieval. This capability is what makes SGE particularly exciting: it promises to offer users not just answers, but nuanced, AI-generated responses that can help guide their search journey in novel and more meaningful directions.

SGE is poised to fundamentally alter how users experience search. Instead of the traditional list of links, users will now be greeted with AI-generated responses that appear above the usual search results. These responses, clearly marked as generated by AI, are designed to provide a quick and comprehensive overview of the queried topic. Google has thoughtfully included citations within these AI-generated answers, allowing users to click through to the original sources for more detailed information. This feature not only enhances the transparency of the information provided but also ensures that the content creators—whose work underpins these AI responses—receive appropriate credit and traffic.

One of the most intriguing aspects of SGE is its conversational mode. In this mode, users can ask follow-up questions naturally, allowing for a more interactive search experience. The AI adapts to the context of each query, refining its understanding of the user's intent and providing increasingly relevant results as the conversation progresses. This conversational approach marks a significant departure from the static nature of traditional search engines, offering a more dynamic and personalised way to explore information.

SGE's application extends beyond general search queries, particularly into specialised areas like shopping and local searches. In the shopping realm, SGE can help users make more informed decisions by presenting detailed product options, complete with descriptions, reviews, ratings, prices, and images—all pulled from Google's expansive Shopping Graph dataset. This capability allows users to explore a wide array of products and make comparisons with ease, enhancing the overall shopping experience. Similarly, for local searches, SGE provides AI-powered insights that enable users to compare local businesses, services, and other options in a streamlined and user-friendly manner.

The introduction of SGE also brings with it important implications for advertisers. While the core functionality of search ads remains intact, SGE will continue to integrate these ads into the search experience, ensuring they appear in relevant slots throughout the page. Google has committed to maintaining transparency in this area, clearly differentiating between ads and organic search results to uphold user trust. This approach underscores Google's ongoing efforts to balance commercial interests with user experience, even as it introduces new technologies.

One of the most exciting potential benefits of SGE is its capacity to unlock new creative possibilities for users. By leveraging generative AI, users can now engage with information in ways that go beyond simple retrieval. Whether it's generating new ideas, drafting content, or exploring creative solutions, SGE offers a powerful toolset for users to harness AI's generative capabilities. However, it's worth noting that, in its initial phase, SGE will impose certain limitations on these creative applications to ensure that quality and safety are prioritised. As the system evolves, we can expect these capabilities to expand, offering even greater creative freedom.

From an SEO perspective, SGE introduces both challenges and opportunities. On the one hand, the rise of AI-generated responses may increase the prevalence of zero-click searches, where users find the information they need directly on the search results page without clicking through to a website. This could potentially reduce traffic to certain types of content. On the other hand, SGE's reliance on trustworthy and authoritative content means that the principles of Experience, Expertise, Authoritativeness, and Trustworthiness (E-E-A-T) will become even more critical. Content that meets these criteria will be more likely to be featured in AI-generated responses, ensuring that high-quality websites continue to receive the visibility and traffic they deserve.

Google's careful and considered approach to implementing SGE is also noteworthy. While the tech industry is often criticised for rushing new AI technologies to market, Google appears to be taking a more measured approach with SGE, emphasising responsible implementation in line with its AI Principles. This commitment to thoughtful development is likely to reassure users and stakeholders who may be concerned about the potential risks associated with generative AI.

The introduction of Google's Search Generative Experience marks a significant leap forward in the evolution of search technology. By integrating generative AI into the search process, Google is not only enhancing the way users find and interact with information but also paving the way for a more dynamic and creative search experience. As SGE continues to develop, it will be fascinating to see how it reshapes the landscape of digital search, offering new possibilities for users, advertisers, and content creators alike. While challenges remain—particularly in balancing the needs of users, businesses, and the ethical considerations of AI—there is no doubt that SGE represents an exciting step into the future of search.

AI for Content

The allure of using AI tools like ChatGPT for generating blog posts and other forms of content has become increasingly tempting. Many businesses and individuals, eager to stay ahead of the curve or simply cut corners, have turned to this powerful AI tool in hopes of streamlining their content creation processes. However, relying on ChatGPT to write your blog posts is akin to bringing a knife to a gunfight—it may seem useful at first glance, but ultimately, it's a losing strategy.

There's no denying the incredible capabilities of AI, and ChatGPT is a prime example of how far this technology has come. It excels at tasks like text completion, language translation, sentiment analysis, and summarising text, making it an invaluable tool for various applications such as chatbots and customer service. In these domains, ChatGPT is indeed a game changer. But when it comes to fuelling your content strategy, particularly for SEO-driven content, ChatGPT falls short. Let me explain why.

It's no surprise that ChatGPT has garnered significant attention within the SEO industry. After all, it's a chatbot that utilises natural language processing to answer questions, potentially making it one of the most widely discussed AI tools to date. However, the excitement surrounding its potential has led to premature conclusions. In the early days of its release, many speculated that AI tools like ChatGPT would soon render human SEOs obsolete—a notion that I find to be completely unfounded. While AI can assist with certain aspects of SEO, such as keyword research and content ideation, it simply cannot replicate the nuanced creativity, emotional depth, and strategic thinking that human writers bring to the table.

What surprises me most is how quickly some people have jumped on the ChatGPT bandwagon without even asking the tool itself if it's suitable for creating original content. If you were to ask ChatGPT, it would candidly tell you that it's not capable of producing genuinely original ideas or content. Instead, it suggests that users conduct their own research and not rely on it as a substitute for human writers. This is a crucial point that many seem to overlook.

Despite these warnings, numerous attempts have been made to generate content—often in bulk—using ChatGPT. The results, however, have been less than stellar. While some of the content may drive traffic, it often fails to attract the right audience or generate meaningful engagement. This is because AI-generated content lacks the personal touch and deep understanding of audience needs that are essential for creating impactful content. For most businesses, especially those without a substantial marketing team or significant revenue, maintaining such content becomes a costly endeavour with little return on investment.

In many ways, the rush to use ChatGPT for content creation mirrors past attempts to use content mills to churn out thousands of low-quality articles at minimal cost. These strategies, rooted in old-school SEO tactics, have repeatedly proven ineffective in driving sustainable business growth. Success in content marketing requires a deep understanding of your audience, a commitment to delivering valuable insights, and the authority to speak on relevant topics. Unfortunately, AI tools like ChatGPT are not yet capable of meeting these requirements.

One of the most glaring issues with relying on AI for content creation is the lack of business acumen among those who advocate for it. High-level content that communicates expertise and addresses consumer concerns cannot be generated by an AI tool, no matter how advanced it may be. The examples of businesses turning to AI for content creation, only to end up with subpar results, are plentiful. A recent Twitter post by a copywriter highlighted this issue, showcasing the grim reality of what happens when businesses place their trust in AI over human writers. The end result is often generic, uninspired content that fails to resonate with its intended audience.

It's important to remember that not all blog posts are created with SEO as the primary goal. Some content is designed to build trust, enhance brand optics, or provide utility to users. Even in these cases, using ChatGPT is unlikely to meet the necessary standards. Content that satisfies Google's expectations—and more importantly, the needs of your audience—requires original information, in-depth analysis, and careful curation. AI-generated content, by its nature, struggles to deliver on these fronts.

Google's algorithms place a premium on content that offers originality, thoroughness, and insightful analysis. The search giant's emphasis on factors like Experience, Expertise, Authoritativeness, and Trustworthiness (E-E-A-T) underscores the importance of high-quality, human-created content. AI tools like ChatGPT, while capable of producing text, cannot replicate the critical thinking, applied knowledge, and originality that are hallmarks of truly valuable content.

Moreover, Google's ranking algorithm evaluates the authority of content by considering the expertise of its authors, the trustworthiness of the website, and the accuracy of the information presented. This level of scrutiny is something that AI-generated content simply cannot withstand. The idea of trusting ChatGPT—or any AI tool—to create content that meets these rigorous standards is not just misguided; it's risky.

ChatGPT should be viewed as a tool, not a solution. It can serve as an effective starting point, particularly when you're struggling with writer's block or need suggestions for sub-topics. However, the responsibility for creating original, thoughtful, and engaging content still lies with human writers. A world filled with AI-generated content is a world where quality and differentiation are sacrificed for convenience. If everyone relies on the same AI tools to produce content, the result is a homogenised landscape where creativity and originality are stifled.

Even if you manage to get AI-generated content indexed by search engines, accuracy remains a significant concern. ChatGPT, while confident in its writing, is often wrong. Its mistakes can range from subtle inaccuracies to glaring factual errors, making it an unreliable source for content that needs to be both informative and trustworthy. In some cases, these errors can be dangerous, particularly if they involve code snippets or other technical information.

So, is using ChatGPT for SEO content generation a good idea? The answer is a resounding no. While it may seem like a convenient option, the lack of differentiation, potential for inaccuracies, and inability to capture the nuances of human thought make it a poor substitute for human creativity and expertise. The hype surrounding AI-generated content may have caused some to lose sight of what truly matters in content creation: originality, relevance, and the ability to connect with your audience on a meaningful level.

When ChatGPT first burst onto the scene, it wasn't long before the internet was flooded with articles claiming, "This was written by ChatGPT!" While some may have found this clever, I found it obnoxious—and more often than not, it was easy to tell that the content was AI-generated. The lack of originality and human touch was evident.

ChatGPT is an impressive tool with a wide range of applications, but content creation is not one of them. The future of SEO and content marketing lies in the hands of those who can blend creativity with expertise, delivering content that is not only optimised for search engines but also resonates with real people. Originality, critical thinking, and a deep understanding of your audience are the keys to success in this field—qualities that AI has yet to master. So, while ChatGPT may be a useful tool in your digital marketing toolkit, it's no replacement for the human touch that makes content truly valuable.

Voice Search

We covered this earlier in the book but voice search is becoming increasingly popular, and optimising for voice queries requires a different approach than traditional text-based SEO.

Natural Language Processing: Voice searches tend to be more conversational and longer than text searches. Optimise your content for natural language queries by incorporating long-tail keywords and answering common questions in a conversational tone.

Featured Snippets: Aim to have your content appear in featured snippets, as these are often used as voice search responses. Providing concise, clear answers to frequently asked questions can increase your chances of being featured.

Local SEO: Many voice searches are location-based, such as users looking for nearby businesses or services. Ensure your local SEO is robust, with accurate business information and strong local citations.

SEO for Connected Devices and IoT

The Internet of Things (IoT) is expanding the range of devices that can access and interact with online content. Optimising for connected devices involves ensuring your content is accessible and user-friendly across a variety of platforms.

Device Compatibility: Ensure your website is compatible with a wide range of devices, including smart speakers, wearables, and connected appliances. This may involve optimising for different screen sizes, interfaces, and input methods.

Structured Data: Use structured data to provide context and improve the discoverability of your content on connected devices. Structured data helps search engines understand the content and purpose of your pages, making it easier for them to deliver relevant information to users.

Performance Optimisation: Connected devices often have varying levels of performance capabilities. Optimise your content to load quickly and efficiently, regardless of the device being used.

SEO for AR and VR

Augmented Reality (AR) and Virtual Reality (VR) are emerging technologies that offer new opportunities for immersive user experiences. Optimising for AR and VR involves creating and promoting content that takes advantage of these technologies.

Content Creation: Develop AR and VR content that provides unique, interactive experiences for users. This could include virtual tours, 3D product demonstrations, or augmented reality applications that enhance real-world experiences.

Technical SEO: Ensure your website is technically optimised to support AR and VR content. This may involve implementing WebXR, optimising for 3D models, and ensuring your site can handle the increased data demands of AR and VR experiences.

Promotion and Integration: Promote your AR and VR content through various channels, including social media, email marketing, and partnerships with AR/VR platforms. Integrate AR and VR experiences into your overall content strategy to enhance user engagement and drive traffic.

By embracing these emerging SEO practices and staying ahead of technological advancements, you can create a comprehensive and future-proof SEO strategy. Leveraging the power of AI, optimising for voice and connected devices, and exploring new frontiers like AR and VR will position your business for success in the ever-evolving digital landscape. Continuously refining your approach and staying updated with the latest trends and best practices will ensure your SEO efforts remain effective and impactful.

CHAPTER 16
SEO & UX

'll broadly repeat some things here that covered in other chapters but I feel it's necessary for those who might want to simply revisit this one. Integrating SEO practices into the User Experience (UX) process is not merely a trend but a necessity in today's digital landscape. For years, SEO and UX were seen as two separate entities—one focused on getting users to the website, the other on ensuring they have a pleasant experience once there. However, as search engines have evolved to prioritise user satisfaction, the lines between SEO and UX have blurred, making it imperative for them to be integrated from the very beginning of the website design and development process. A website that ranks well but frustrates users will ultimately fail to achieve its objectives, just as a website that provides an excellent user experience but is invisible in search engine results will struggle to attract the necessary traffic. This chapter delves deeply into the symbiotic relationship between SEO and UX, explaining why they must work together and offering practical strategies for seamless integration.

The Symbiotic Relationship Between SEO and UX

Understanding the relationship between SEO and UX is the first step toward successful integration. SEO, at its core, is about making your website more visible to search engines. It involves optimising your site so that it can be easily found and understood by search engines like Google, which then rank it according to its relevance to user queries. UX, on the other hand, is about how users interact with your site. It's about ensuring that once users arrive, they can easily find what they need, engage with your content, and achieve their goals without frustration.

In the past, these two disciplines often worked in silos, with SEO focusing on technical aspects like keywords and backlinks, and UX concentrating on design and usability. But as search engines have become more sophisticated, they have begun to prioritise user experience as a key ranking factor. Google, for instance, uses metrics like bounce rate, time on site, and mobile usability to help determine where a site should rank. This means that a well-optimised site that offers a poor user experience is unlikely to perform well in search rankings. Conversely, a site with excellent UX but poor SEO might not attract the traffic it deserves. Therefore, to succeed in today's competitive digital landscape, SEO and UX must work hand in hand.

Consider, for example, a website that loads slowly and is difficult to navigate. Even if it is optimised with the right keywords and has strong backlinks, users are likely to leave if they find it frustrating to use. This high bounce rate will signal to search engines that the site is not providing a good user experience, leading to a drop in rankings. On the other hand, a site that is fast, easy to navigate, and provides relevant, high-quality content will keep users engaged, leading to better SEO performance.

The key to integrating SEO and UX lies in recognising that they both share the same ultimate goal: to satisfy the user's needs. When a user types a query into a search engine, they are looking for information, solutions, or products. It is the job of SEO to ensure that your site appears in the search results for that query. Once the user clicks through to your site, it is the job of UX to ensure that they find what they are looking for quickly and easily, and that their experience is so positive that they want to return. By integrating SEO and UX, you can create a website that not only attracts visitors but also keeps them coming back.

To fully integrate SEO into the UX design process, it's important to consider SEO principles at every stage of design and development. This ensures that the site is built with both search engines and users in mind, leading to a more cohesive and effective online presence.

Keyword Research as a Foundation for Information Architecture

Keyword research is one of the cornerstones of SEO. It involves identifying the terms and phrases that users are searching for in relation to your content, products, or services. However, keyword research should not be seen as just an SEO activity; it should also inform the Information Architecture (IA) of your site. IA refers to the way content is organised and structured, making it easy for users to find what they're looking for.

By aligning IA with keyword research, you can ensure that your site's navigation and content structure reflect the language and expectations of your users. This approach not only helps with SEO but also makes it easier for users to find relevant information quickly. For example, if keyword research reveals that users frequently search for "affordable web design services," you should ensure that this phrase and related terms are integrated into your site's navigation, headings, and content. This not only helps your site rank for those terms but also makes it easier for users who are looking for that specific service to find it quickly.

When structuring your site's navigation, consider the most logical and intuitive way for users to find information. For example, a user looking for "affordable web design services" might first look for a category like "Services" and then drill down into more specific subcategories. By aligning your navigation with the way users think and search, you create a seamless experience that guides users to the information they need while also helping search engines understand the structure of your site.

On-Page SEO and Content Design: Creating Engaging, Accessible Content

On-page SEO involves optimising individual pages to rank higher in search results and attract more relevant traffic. Key on-page SEO elements include title tags, meta descriptions, headings, and alt text for images. These elements are not just for search engines; they also play a crucial role in UX.

Title tags and meta descriptions, for example, are often the first things users see in search engine results. A well-crafted title tag and meta description can entice users to click through to your site. Once they arrive, headings and subheadings help users scan the page and find the information they need quickly. Alt text for images not only helps with accessibility for users who rely on screen readers but also provides additional context for search engines, improving your chances of ranking in image searches.

When creating content, it's important to focus on both relevance and readability. Relevance means ensuring that your content addresses the needs and interests of your target audience. This requires a deep understanding of your users, which can be gained through user research, analytics, and customer feedback. Readability, on the other hand, involves presenting your content in a way that is easy to consume. This includes using clear, concise language, breaking up text with headings and bullet points, and incorporating visual elements such as images and videos to enhance understanding.

Page Load Speed and Performance Optimisation

Page load speed is a critical factor for both SEO and UX. Users expect web pages to load quickly, and if they don't, they are likely to leave and look elsewhere. Google has made it clear that page speed is a ranking factor, so slow-loading pages can hurt your SEO efforts.

To optimise page load speed, consider using techniques such as image compression, browser caching, and minimising the use of heavy scripts. It's also important to choose a reliable web hosting service and implement a content delivery network (CDN) if necessary. By prioritising page speed in the UX design process, you not only improve user satisfaction but also boost your site's SEO performance.

In addition to technical optimisations, consider the impact of your design choices on page load speed. For example, while large, high-resolution images and videos can enhance the visual appeal of your site, they can also significantly slow down page load times if not properly optimised. Similarly, complex animations and interactive elements may look impressive, but if they cause your site to load slowly, they may do more harm than good. By striking a balance between aesthetics and performance, you can create a site that is both visually appealing and fast-loading, providing a positive experience for users and improving your SEO.

Mobile Optimisation and Responsive Design

With the majority of web traffic now coming from mobile devices, mobile optimisation is more important than ever. Google has shifted to mobile-first indexing, meaning that the mobile version of your site is considered the primary version for ranking purposes. This makes it essential to ensure that your site is fully optimised for mobile users.

Responsive design is a key component of mobile optimisation. A responsive site automatically adjusts its layout and design to fit the screen size of the device being used, providing a seamless experience across desktops, tablets, and smartphones. In addition to responsive design, other mobile optimisation strategies include simplifying navigation, using larger touch targets for buttons and links, and ensuring that content is easily readable without zooming.

But mobile optimisation goes beyond just design. It also involves considering how mobile users interact with your content and ensuring that your site meets their needs. For example, mobile users are often looking for quick answers or specific information, so it's important to prioritise content that is relevant to their needs and easy to access on a small screen. This might involve rethinking your content hierarchy, placing the most important information at the top of the page, and using concise, scannable text that can be easily read on a mobile device.

Navigation and Site Structure: Simplifying the User Journey

A well-structured site with intuitive navigation is essential for both UX and SEO. Users should be able to find what they're looking for quickly and easily, without having to click through multiple pages or guess where content is located. At the same time, a clear site structure helps search engines crawl and index your site more effectively.

When designing navigation, consider the following best practices: Use clear, descriptive labels for navigation links; ensure that the most important pages are easily accessible from the homepage; and implement breadcrumb navigation to help users understand their location within the site. Additionally, avoid using too many layers of navigation, as this can make it difficult for both users and search engines to find content.

It's also important to consider the needs of different types of users when designing your site's navigation. For example, a first-time visitor to your site might be looking for general information about your products or services, while a returning customer might be looking for specific details about a recent purchase or account information. By designing navigation that caters to the needs of both new and returning users, you can create a more personalised and effective user experiences. This, in turn, enhances your SEO by ensuring that users are able to find what they need quickly and efficiently, leading to lower bounce rates, higher engagement, and better overall site performance.

SEO and UX in User Testing

One of the most powerful ways to integrate SEO into the UX process is through user testing. User testing involves observing real users as they interact with your site, allowing you to identify areas of confusion or frustration and make improvements based on real-world feedback. While user testing has traditionally been focused on usability, it can also provide valuable insights for SEO.

For example, during user testing, you might discover that users are having trouble finding a particular piece of content because the language used in your navigation or headings doesn't match the terms they're searching for. This could indicate a disconnect between your keyword strategy and the way users actually think and search. By aligning your content with the language and mental models of your users, you can improve both the usability of your site and its relevance to search queries, leading to better SEO performance.

User testing can also help you identify technical SEO issues that might be affecting the user experience. For instance, if users are consistently experiencing slow load times or encountering broken links, these issues are likely to be affecting your SEO as well. By addressing these issues as part of the UX testing process, you can create a site that is both user-friendly and optimised for search engines.

In addition to traditional user testing, other UX methodologies such as A/B testing and heat mapping can also be used to optimise for both SEO and UX. A/B testing involves comparing two versions of a page to see which one performs better in terms of user engagement and conversions. By testing different variations of page elements such as headlines, images, and calls to action, you can determine which version is more effective at keeping users engaged and driving conversions. This not only improves the user experience but can also have a positive impact on SEO by reducing bounce rates and increasing time on site.

Heat mapping, on the other hand, allows you to see where users are clicking, scrolling, and spending the most time on your pages. This can provide valuable insights into how users are interacting with your content and whether there are any areas of your site that are being overlooked. For example, if you notice that users are not clicking on a particular call to action, it might be because it's not positioned prominently enough or because the wording is unclear. By making adjustments based on heat map data, you can improve both the usability of your site and its SEO performance. Be cautious here though, do not assume that users are clicking on something for the right reasons – it might be click rage due to something that's not working. Use heatmaps in conjunction with User testing only.

Content Strategy: Marrying SEO with User Needs

Content is at the heart of both SEO and UX, and creating a content strategy that marries the two is essential for success. SEO-driven content strategies often focus on targeting specific keywords and optimising for search engines, while UX-driven content strategies prioritise the needs and interests of the user. However, the most effective content strategies are those that balance both SEO and UX considerations, ensuring that content is not only optimised for search engines but also resonates with users and provides real value.

To achieve this balance, start by conducting thorough keyword research to identify the terms and phrases your target audience is searching for. However, instead of focusing solely on high-volume keywords, consider the intent behind those searches. Are users looking for information, solutions to a problem, or a specific product or service? By understanding the intent behind search queries, you can create content that not only ranks well in search results but also meets the needs of your users.

Once you've identified your target keywords, use them strategically throughout your content, but avoid keyword stuffing. Instead, focus on creating content that is relevant, informative, and engaging. This might involve creating in-depth guides, how-to articles, case studies, or other types of content that provide real value to your audience. Remember that search engines like Google are increasingly prioritising content that demonstrates expertise, authoritativeness, and trustworthiness (E-E-A-T), so it's important to create content that reflects these qualities.

In addition to optimising your content for search engines, it's also important to consider the user experience. This means presenting your content in a way that is easy to read and navigate, using clear headings, bullet points, and images to break up text and enhance understanding. It also means ensuring that your content is accessible to all users, including those with disabilities, by providing alt text for images, captions for videos, and ensuring that your site is navigable by keyboard.

Another important aspect of integrating SEO into your content strategy is the use of internal linking. Internal links help search engines understand the structure of your site and the relationships between different pieces of content. They also help users navigate your site, making it easier for them to find related content and explore your offerings. When creating content, look for opportunities to link to other relevant pages on your site, using descriptive anchor text that includes your target keywords.

Micro-Moments: Aligning SEO and UX for Immediate User Satisfaction

In today's fast-paced digital world, users often turn to their devices for quick answers and immediate solutions. These "micro-moments" occur when users need to know something, go somewhere, do something, or buy something. Google has identified these micro-moments as critical touchpoints in the customer journey, and they present a unique opportunity for aligning SEO and UX.

To capitalise on micro-moments, it's important to create content that addresses users' immediate needs and provides quick, actionable answers. This might involve creating FAQ pages, how-to guides, or short, informative blog posts that answer common questions related to your products or services. By creating content that is optimised for these micro-moments, you can ensure that your site appears in search results when users are looking for quick answers, and that the content they find is easy to consume and act upon.

In addition to creating content for micro-moments, it's also important to consider the user experience. Users in these moments are often looking for quick answers and are unlikely to spend a lot of time navigating through a complex site. To meet their needs, ensure that your content is easily accessible from your homepage or main navigation, and that it is presented in a clear, concise format that allows users to find the information they need quickly.

Technical SEO and UX: Building a Foundation for Success

While much of the focus on integrating SEO and UX revolves around content and design, it's also important to consider the technical aspects of your site. Technical SEO involves optimising the backend of your site to ensure that it is easily crawled and indexed by search engines, while also providing a smooth and seamless user experience.

One of the most important aspects of technical SEO is ensuring that your site is mobile-friendly. With the majority of web traffic now coming from mobile devices, it's essential that your site is optimised for mobile users. This means using responsive design to ensure that your site adjusts to different screen sizes, as well as optimising page load times and minimising the use of heavy scripts and images that can slow down performance.

Another important aspect of technical SEO is ensuring that your site is secure. Google has made it clear that site security is a ranking factor, and users are also more likely to trust and engage with sites that are secure. To ensure that your site is secure, make sure that you have an SSL certificate installed, and that your site is served over HTTPS.

Site speed is another critical factor in both SEO and UX. Users expect sites to load quickly, and slow-loading pages can lead to higher bounce rates and lower engagement. To optimise site speed, consider using techniques such as image compression, browser caching, and minimising the use of heavy scripts. Additionally, consider using a content delivery network (CDN) to ensure that your site loads quickly for users around the world.

The Interplay Between SEO, UX, and Conversion Rate Optimisation (CRO)

Conversion Rate Optimisation (CRO) is the process of optimising your site to increase the percentage of visitors who take a desired action, such as making a purchase, signing up for a newsletter, or filling out a contact form. While CRO is often seen as a separate discipline from SEO and UX, there is a significant overlap between these areas, and integrating them can lead to powerful results.

At the intersection of SEO, UX, and CRO is the idea that every element of your site should be designed to guide users towards a specific goal, whether that's making a purchase, signing up for a newsletter, or simply staying on your site longer. This means that your content, design, and technical SEO elements should all work together to create a seamless and persuasive user journey.

For example, a well-optimised landing page might use targeted keywords to attract search traffic, while also featuring a clear, compelling headline and a strong call to action that encourages users to take the next step. The page might also be designed with CRO principles in mind, using persuasive copy, social proof, and trust signals to build confidence and encourage conversions.

By integrating SEO, UX, and CRO, you can create a site that not only attracts visitors but also converts them into customers or leads. This holistic approach ensures that your site is not only visible in search results but also provides a positive user experience that drives business results.

Prioritising Accessibility in SEO and UX Integration

Accessibility is another critical consideration when integrating SEO and UX. Accessible websites are designed to be usable by people with a wide range of abilities, including those with visual, auditory, motor, or cognitive disabilities. While accessibility is often considered a UX issue, it also has significant implications for SEO.

For example, using alt text for images not only helps visually impaired users understand the content of an image but also provides additional context for search engines, improving your chances of ranking in image searches. Similarly, using descriptive headings and clear, concise language can make your content more accessible to users with cognitive disabilities, while also helping search engines understand the structure and relevance of your content.

By prioritising accessibility in your SEO and UX integration efforts, you can create a site that is inclusive and user-friendly for all visitors while also improving your search engine rankings. This not only helps you reach a broader audience but also demonstrates a commitment to inclusivity, which can enhance your brand reputation and trustworthiness.

Understanding User Intent: A Shared Goal for SEO and UX

One of the most critical aspects of integrating SEO and UX is understanding user intent. User intent refers to the goal or purpose behind a user's search query—what they are looking to accomplish or find when they enter a query into a search engine. Understanding and addressing user intent is key to both SEO success and delivering a satisfying user experience.

From an SEO perspective, aligning your content with user intent ensures that your pages are relevant to the queries users are searching for. Search engines like Google have become increasingly adept at interpreting user intent, which means that content must be closely aligned with what users are actually looking for. This requires a deep understanding of the different types of search intent, which generally fall into four categories: informational, navigational, transactional, and commercial investigation.

For example, a user searching for "how to fix a leaky tap" likely has informational intent—they are looking for a guide or tutorial. On the other hand, someone searching for "buy kitchen faucets online" has transactional intent—they are ready to make a purchase. Understanding the intent behind these queries allows you to create content that not only ranks well but also meets the specific needs of the user.

From a UX perspective, understanding user intent helps ensure that once users arrive on your site, they can quickly and easily find the information or solutions they're looking for. This means designing your site and organising your content in a way that aligns with the user's journey. For example, if a user's intent is informational, they should be able to find clear, detailed content that answers their questions without having to sift through unrelated product pages. Conversely, if their intent is transactional, your site should make it easy for them to find the products they're looking for and complete their purchase with minimal friction.

By integrating an understanding of user intent into both your SEO and UX strategies, you can create a seamless experience that starts with the user's search query and continues through their journey on your site. This not only improves your chances of ranking well in search results but also increases the likelihood that users will find what they need, leading to higher engagement and conversion rates.

The Role of Content in Bridging SEO and UX

Content serves as the bridge between SEO and UX, playing a crucial role in both attracting visitors to your site and keeping them engaged once they arrive. To effectively integrate SEO and UX, it's important to adopt a content-first approach—one that prioritises the creation of high-quality, relevant content that meets the needs of both search engines and users.

This means moving beyond a narrow focus on keywords and instead creating content that provides real value. It involves understanding your audience's pain points, questions, and needs, and creating content that addresses these directly. Whether it's a blog post, product description, or landing page, every piece of content on your site should be crafted with both SEO and UX in mind.

For SEO, this means ensuring that your content is optimised with relevant keywords, meta tags, and structured data to improve its visibility in search engine results. But equally important is ensuring that the content is engaging, easy to read, and provides a clear path for users to follow. This might involve breaking up text with subheadings and bullet points, using images and videos to enhance understanding, and including clear calls to action that guide users toward their next step.

Incorporating multimedia content, such as videos, infographics, and interactive elements, can also enhance both SEO and UX. Multimedia content is highly engaging and can help to keep users on your site longer, which can improve your SEO metrics such as dwell time and reduce bounce rates. Additionally, search engines increasingly favour content that includes rich media, as it provides a more dynamic and informative user experience.

Continuous Improvement: The Role of Analytics in SEO and UX

A successful integration of SEO and UX requires a commitment to continuous improvement, driven by data and analytics. By regularly monitoring and analysing user behaviour, you can identify areas where your SEO and UX strategies are working well, as well as areas that need improvement.

Tools like Google Analytics, heat maps, and user session recordings provide valuable insights into how users are interacting with your site. For example, if you notice that a particular page has a high bounce rate, it may indicate that the content is not meeting user expectations or that the page is difficult to navigate. Conversely, pages with high engagement and conversion rates can provide clues about what is working well and should be replicated across your site.

A/B testing is another powerful tool for optimising both SEO and UX. By testing different versions of a page or element, such as a headline, call to action, or layout, you can determine which version performs better in terms of user engagement and conversions. This iterative approach allows you to make data-driven decisions that enhance both the user experience and your SEO performance.

In addition to analysing user behaviour on your site, it's also important to monitor your site's performance in search engine rankings. SEO tools like SEMrush, Ahrefs, and Moz can provide insights into how your site is ranking for target keywords, as well as how your competitors are performing. By tracking your rankings over time, you can identify trends and make adjustments to your strategy as needed.

One key area to monitor is the impact of any changes you make to your site on both SEO and UX metrics. For example, if you redesign a key landing page, you'll want to track how this affects both your search engine rankings and user engagement metrics. If you see improvements in both areas, this indicates that the redesign was successful. If not, you may need to revisit your design and content strategy to better align with user needs and search engine requirements.

Building a Collaborative Team: The Intersection of SEO, UX, and Development

To successfully integrate SEO into the UX process, it's essential to foster collaboration between the SEO, UX, and development teams. Each of these teams brings a unique perspective and set of skills to the table, and by working together, they can create a site that is optimised for both search engines and users.

For example, the SEO team can provide insights into how users are searching for content and what keywords should be targeted, while the UX team can ensure that the site is designed to meet the needs of those users once they arrive. The development team, on the other hand, can implement the technical optimisations needed to ensure that the site is fast, secure, and accessible.

Regular communication and collaboration between these teams are key to ensuring that SEO and UX are integrated effectively. This might involve joint planning sessions, regular check-ins, and collaborative testing and optimisation efforts. By working together, these teams can create a site that is not only visible in search results but also provides a seamless and satisfying experience for users.

The Future of SEO and UX Integration

As search engines continue to evolve and place greater emphasis on user experience, the integration of SEO and UX will become increasingly important. Emerging technologies such as artificial intelligence, voice search, and augmented reality are likely to further blur the lines between these disciplines, making it essential for SEO and UX to work together in new and innovative ways.

For example, as voice search becomes more prevalent, the focus will shift from traditional keyword optimisation to optimising for natural language queries and conversational interactions. This will require a deep understanding of user intent and the ability to create content that not only answers questions but does so in a way that is clear, concise, and easy to understand when spoken.

Similarly, the rise of AI-driven search engines and personalised search experiences will place even greater emphasis on delivering content that is tailored to the individual needs and preferences of users. This will require a more nuanced approach to both SEO and UX, with a focus on creating dynamic, personalised experiences that can adapt to the changing needs of users.

As these trends continue to develop, the need for a holistic, integrated approach to SEO and UX will only grow. By staying ahead of these changes and continuously refining your strategy, you can create a site that not only ranks well in search results but also provides a superior user experience that keeps visitors coming back.

Integrating SEO practices into the UX process is essential for creating a website that is both visible in search engines and engaging for users. By focusing on the shared goal of meeting user needs, aligning content with user intent, and leveraging data-driven insights, you can create a site that not only attracts visitors but also converts them into loyal customers. The future of digital marketing lies in the seamless integration of SEO and UX, and those who embrace this approach will be well-positioned to succeed in an increasingly competitive online landscape.

CHAPTER 17

ETHICS AND COMPLIANCE IN SEO

In the ever-evolving world of SEO, ethics and compliance are paramount. As search engines become more sophisticated, maintaining ethical practices not only ensures long-term success but also builds trust with users and search engines alike. This chapter delves into the importance of ethical SEO practices, the necessity of adhering to regulatory standards, strategies for recovering from algorithm penalties, and techniques for analysing competitors within ethical boundaries.

Ethical SEO practices are fundamental to sustaining a reputable and effective online presence. The distinction between White Hat and Black Hat SEO is crucial in understanding what constitutes ethical behaviour in the SEO industry.

White Hat vs. Black Hat SEO

White Hat SEO refers to optimisation strategies that adhere to search engine guidelines and focus on providing value to users. These practices include producing high-quality content, optimising website performance, ensuring a great user experience, and earning backlinks through legitimate means. White Hat SEO is about building a sustainable online presence through integrity and transparency.

Black Hat SEO, on the other hand, involves tactics that attempt to manipulate search engine algorithms and often violate their terms of service. These practices include keyword stuffing, cloaking, using private link networks, and other deceptive techniques designed to achieve quick, short-term gains. While Black Hat tactics may yield temporary success, they often result in severe penalties from search engines, including loss of rankings or complete removal from search results. One common form of Black Hat SEO is paid-for links. If someone offers to get you a tonne of links and it seems too good to be true, then trust me.. it is.

With the rise of AI in SEO, the ethical considerations have extended to how AI is used in optimisation practices. Ethical use of AI involves leveraging its capabilities to enhance user experience, analyse data more effectively, and predict trends without compromising integrity. AI should be used to support White Hat strategies, ensuring transparency and fairness in SEO efforts .

Regulatory Compliance

In addition to ethical practices, SEO professionals must navigate a complex landscape of regulatory requirements. Adhering to legal standards not only protects your business from penalties but also builds trust with your audience. The General Data Protection Regulation (GDPR) is one of the most significant regulatory frameworks impacting SEO and digital marketing. GDPR mandates strict guidelines on how personal data is collected, stored, and used. Compliance with GDPR involves:

- Obtaining explicit consent from users before collecting their data.

- Ensuring data is stored securely and used only for its intended purpose.

- Providing users with access to their data and the ability to request its deletion.

- Implementing clear privacy policies and making them easily accessible to users.

Beyond GDPR, other regulations such as the California Consumer Privacy Act (CCPA) and various international standards must be adhered to. Compliance with these regulations demonstrates a commitment to protecting user privacy and maintaining ethical standards in data handling.

Algorithm Penalties and Recoveries

Despite best efforts, websites can sometimes fall foul of search engine algorithms and incur penalties. Understanding how to navigate and recover from these penalties is crucial for maintaining a healthy online presence. Search engine penalties can occur for various reasons, including the use of Black Hat tactics, poor-quality content, and technical issues. There are two main types of penalties: manual and algorithmic.

Manual Penalties: These are imposed by human reviewers at search engines when they identify a violation of guidelines. Common reasons include unnatural links, thin content, and cloaking. To recover from a manual penalty:

• Identify the cause of the penalty using tools like Google Search Console.

• Correct the issues, such as removing unnatural links or improving content quality.

• Submit a reconsideration request to the search engine, detailing the steps taken to rectify the problems.

Algorithmic Penalties: These are automatic penalties applied by search engine algorithms when they detect issues like keyword stuffing or duplicate content. Recovering from algorithmic penalties involves:

• Conducting a thorough site audit to identify and rectify issues.

• Improving content quality and ensuring it meets E-E-A-T (Experience, Expertise, Authoritativeness, Trustworthiness) standards.

• Monitoring performance using analytics tools to ensure ongoing compliance with search engine guidelines.

Staying updated with search engine algorithm changes and regularly auditing your site can help prevent penalties and ensure quick recovery if they occur.

Competitive Analysis

Understanding the competitive landscape is essential for developing effective SEO strategies. However, competitive analysis should be conducted ethically and within the bounds of fair play. Competitive analysis involves examining the strategies and performance of your competitors to identify opportunities and areas for improvement. Here are some techniques for ethical competitive analysis:

Keyword Analysis: Identify the keywords your competitors are ranking for and assess their relevance to your own SEO strategy. Tools like SEMrush and Ahrefs can provide insights into keyword performance and competition.

Content Analysis: Evaluate the content strategies of your competitors, including the types of content they produce, their quality, and engagement levels. Identify gaps in their content that you can fill with high-quality, relevant content.

Backlink Analysis: Analyse the backlink profiles of your competitors to understand their link-building strategies. Identify high-quality sites that link to your competitors and consider how you might earn similar backlinks through White Hat techniques.

Technical SEO Audit: Conduct a technical audit of your competitors' websites to identify strengths and weaknesses. Look at site speed, mobile-friendliness, and other technical factors that impact SEO performance.

Social Media Presence: Examine the social media strategies of your competitors, including their engagement levels, content types, and follower growth. Understanding their social media tactics can inform your own strategies for integrating social signals into your SEO efforts.

By conducting thorough and ethical competitive analysis, you can gain valuable insights that inform your SEO strategies while maintaining the integrity and fairness expected in the industry.

Ethics and compliance are foundational to successful and sustainable SEO practices. By adhering to ethical guidelines, complying with regulatory standards, effectively managing algorithm penalties, and conducting competitive analysis ethically, you can build a robust SEO strategy that not only improves rankings but also fosters trust and credibility with users and search engines alike. Embracing these principles ensures long-term success and positions your brand as a responsible and trustworthy leader in the digital space.

CHAPTER 18
HIDING DEAD BODIES

No, I don't kill people. Instead I refer to using SEO to demote negative news stories or unwanted search results.

Managing your online reputation is more important than ever. The prominence of negative news stories or unwanted search results can have a profound impact on both individuals and businesses. Whether it's a damaging news article, a negative review, or other unfavourable content, these results can surface prominently in search engine rankings, potentially harming your reputation, credibility, and bottom line. However, through strategic use of SEO techniques, it's possible to demote these negative results, pushing them lower in search engine rankings where they are less likely to be seen.

Understanding the Challenge

Before diving into strategies for demoting negative content, it's important to understand the challenge. Search engines, especially Google, are designed to deliver the most relevant and authoritative results to users. If a negative news story or unwanted result ranks highly, it's often because the content is considered by the search engine to be highly relevant, credible, or frequently visited by users.

Given this, the goal of using SEO to manage negative content isn't about "tricking" search engines. Instead, it's about providing better, more relevant content that aligns with what users are genuinely searching for. By creating and optimising positive content, you can gradually shift the search engine's perception of what is most relevant and valuable, thereby pushing negative results lower in the rankings.

Building a Positive Online Presence

The foundation of any strategy to demote negative search results is to build a strong, positive online presence. This involves creating high-quality, authoritative content that is aligned with your personal or business brand. Start by identifying the key topics or keywords that are most relevant to you or your business. These should be terms that you want to be associated with, rather than the negative content you are trying to demote.

Content creation should be approached strategically. This means not only focusing on the quantity of content but also its quality and relevance. Create a variety of content types, including blog posts, articles, press releases, social media posts, videos, and infographics. The goal is to flood the search engine index with positive, relevant content that can outrank the negative results.

One of the most effective ways to create authoritative content is through a blog or a dedicated section on your website. Regularly publishing well-researched, high-quality articles on topics relevant to your audience can help establish your website as a go-to source for information. Ensure that these articles are optimised for SEO, with relevant keywords, meta tags, and internal links that reinforce the content's relevance.

Another important aspect of building a positive online presence is to leverage your social media profiles. Social media platforms are often highly ranked by search engines, so regularly updating your profiles with positive content, news, and updates can help push negative results down. Consistent, positive engagement on social media can also signal to search engines that your brand is active and authoritative.

Optimising Existing Positive Content

In addition to creating new content, it's crucial to optimise any existing positive content that might not be performing as well as it could in search rankings. This includes revisiting older blog posts, articles, and web pages to ensure they are fully optimised for SEO. Start by conducting an audit of your current content to identify which pages are already ranking but could potentially rank higher with some optimisation.

Enhance the on-page SEO of these pages by updating titles, meta descriptions, and header tags to include relevant keywords. Ensure that the content is still current and accurate, and make any necessary updates to improve its relevance. Additionally, consider adding new internal links to these pages from other parts of your website to help boost their SEO value.

If you have any content that is already ranking well for certain keywords, focus on amplifying its visibility. This could involve promoting the content through social media, building backlinks, or even repurposing it into other formats like videos or infographics. The more exposure this positive content receives, the more likely it is to outrank negative results.

Leveraging Third-Party Websites

Third-party websites, particularly those with high domain authority, can be powerful allies in your quest to demote negative search results. Consider publishing guest posts, articles, or press releases on reputable websites that are relevant to your industry. These external sites often have a strong presence in search engine results, which can help push down negative content related to your brand.

When creating content for third-party sites, ensure that it is well-optimised for SEO and includes backlinks to your website or other positive content. These backlinks can help boost the authority of your own site, while also increasing the likelihood that the third-party content will rank well.

You can also consider creating profiles on professional or industry-specific directories and review sites. These profiles, if well-optimised, can rank highly in search results for your brand name or other relevant keywords. The more high-ranking positive content that exists, the more difficult it becomes for negative results to maintain a prominent position.

Using Local SEO and Google Business Profile

For businesses, local SEO is a critical component of managing online reputation. Local search results often include not only websites but also Google Business Profile (GBP), reviews, and local directories. Optimising your GBP can help ensure that positive information about your business is prominently displayed in local search results.

Start by claiming and fully optimising your GBP. This includes providing complete and accurate information about your business, including your address, phone number, business hours, and services offered. Regularly update your profile with new photos, posts, and offers to keep it active and engaging.

Encourage satisfied customers to leave positive reviews on your GBP and other local review sites. Positive reviews can help counteract negative content and improve your overall online reputation. Respond to reviews promptly, whether they are positive or negative, to show that you are engaged and responsive to customer feedback.

Managing Negative Reviews and Feedback

Negative reviews and feedback are common issues that can impact search results. While it's not always possible to remove negative reviews, there are strategies for managing them effectively. The first step is to respond professionally and constructively to any negative feedback. Address the reviewer's concerns, offer solutions, and show that you are committed to improving the customer experience.

In some cases, it may be possible to have negative reviews removed if they violate the terms and conditions of the review platform. For example, reviews that are defamatory, fraudulent, or irrelevant may be eligible for removal. However, this should be approached carefully, as attempting to remove legitimate reviews can backfire and damage your reputation further.

Another strategy is to encourage satisfied customers to leave positive reviews. The more positive reviews you have, the less impact negative ones will have on your overall rating. Additionally, a steady stream of new positive reviews can push older negative reviews further down the list, making them less visible to potential customers.

Employing Advanced SEO Techniques

For more persistent or damaging negative content, advanced SEO techniques may be required. One such technique is the creation of a microsite or multiple microsites focused on specific keywords or topics. These microsites can be optimised to rank highly in search results, pushing negative content further down the rankings.

Another advanced technique is to use strategic link building to enhance the authority of your positive content. This involves obtaining high-quality backlinks from reputable websites to your positive content. The more authoritative backlinks you have, the more likely your content is to rank well, thereby demoting negative results.

You can also use content syndication to distribute your positive content across multiple platforms. Syndicating your content to news sites, blogs, and other online platforms can increase its visibility and authority. This not only helps push negative content down but also ensures that your positive content reaches a wider audience.

Monitoring and Continuous Improvement

The process of demoting negative content is not a one-time effort but requires ongoing monitoring and adjustments. Regularly track your search engine rankings to see how your efforts are affecting the placement of negative content. Use tools like Google Alerts, SEMrush, or Ahrefs to stay informed about any new mentions of your brand or changes in search rankings.

If negative content starts to resurface, revisit your strategy and make adjustments as needed. This might involve creating new content, building additional backlinks, or optimising existing content further.

The key is to remain proactive and vigilant, ensuring that positive content consistently outperforms negative content in search results.

Continuous improvement also means staying informed about the latest SEO trends and best practices. Search engine algorithms are constantly evolving, and what works today may not be as effective tomorrow. By staying up-to-date with the latest developments in SEO, you can adapt your strategies to maintain a positive online presence.

Finally, it's important to understand that demoting negative content is a gradual process that requires patience and persistence. SEO is not an overnight solution, and it may take time to see significant results. However, by consistently applying the strategies outlined in this chapter, you can gradually push negative content down in search rankings and improve your online reputation.

Remember that the ultimate goal is not just to hide negative content but to build a strong, positive online presence that reflects the true value of your brand. By focusing on creating and promoting high-quality, authoritative content, you can ensure that your brand is represented in the best possible light, regardless of what negative content may exist.

CHAPTER 19
REPORTING ON SEO EFFORTS

The world of SEO is in a constant state of flux, shaped by the evolution of search engine algorithms, changes in user behaviour, and the ongoing development of digital analytics tools. As these factors continue to evolve, so too must our approach to reporting on SEO efforts. In this chapter, we will explore the complexities of SEO reporting in the current environment, focusing on the challenges posed by the shift to Google Analytics 4 (GA4) and the strategies that can be employed to overcome these obstacles. We will also delve into the use of Google Search Console (GSC) and third-party tools such as SEMrush to provide a comprehensive view of SEO performance. Finally, we will discuss the importance of projecting potential traffic gains based on search volume data and ranking improvements, offering insights into how to quantify and communicate the impact of SEO initiatives.

The introduction of Google Analytics 4 represents a significant shift in how digital marketers approach data analysis and reporting. Unlike its predecessor, Universal Analytics, GA4 emphasises a user-centric approach, focusing on events and user interactions rather than the traditional keyword-centric model. This transition has introduced new challenges for SEO professionals who have long relied on detailed keyword data to measure the success of their optimisation efforts. In GA4, keyword-level insights are no longer as readily available, requiring marketers to adopt new strategies for interpreting and reporting on SEO performance.

One of the key changes in GA4 is its focus on engagement metrics. Rather than simply tracking pageviews or bounce rates, GA4 provides deeper insights into how users interact with your content. Metrics such as average engagement time, user journey flow, and event tracking allow you to understand how visitors navigate your site and engage with different elements. These metrics are crucial for SEO reporting, as they offer a more holistic view of how well your content is resonating with your audience. By analysing these engagement metrics, you can infer which types of content are driving the most value, even in the absence of direct keyword data. For example, a landing page with high engagement and conversion rates might indicate that the content is effectively addressing the needs of users, even if the specific search queries that brought them there are not visible in GA4.

Despite the reduced availability of keyword data in GA4, Google Search Console remains an essential tool for understanding and reporting on SEO performance. GSC provides direct access to valuable search query data, allowing you to see which keywords are driving traffic to your site. This data, combined with information on impressions, clicks, and average positions, gives you a detailed picture of how your site is performing in search results. By integrating GSC data into your SEO reports, you can compensate for the gaps left by GA4, ensuring that you maintain a granular understanding of keyword performance.

GSC also allows you to track trends over time, providing insights into how your SEO efforts are impacting search visibility. For instance, if you notice that a particular keyword is gaining more impressions but has a low click-through rate (CTR), this could indicate that your meta descriptions or titles need optimisation. Conversely, a keyword with high CTR but low impressions might suggest an opportunity to improve the content or increase its visibility. These insights are invaluable for fine-tuning your SEO strategy and ensuring that your content continues to perform well in organic search.

In addition to GA4 and GSC, third-party tools like SEMrush can significantly enhance your SEO reporting by providing metrics that offer a broader view of your website's performance within the competitive landscape. SEMrush, for example, provides visibility and Share of Voice (SOV) metrics, which are particularly useful for understanding how your site compares to competitors in search results. Visibility metrics indicate how prominently your site appears across a range of keywords, offering insights into your overall search presence. A high visibility score suggests that your site is well-positioned to attract organic traffic, while a lower score might indicate the need for further optimisation.

Share of Voice, on the other hand, measures your site's dominance in search results relative to competitors. This metric provides a competitive perspective, showing how much of the search landscape your site commands for specific keywords or topics. By regularly monitoring your Share of Voice, you can identify shifts in your competitive position and uncover opportunities to increase your market share. For example, if you notice that a competitor is gaining ground on a particular keyword, you might decide to focus your efforts on improving content or building more backlinks to regain your lead. These competitive insights are crucial for maintaining and improving your site's visibility in search results, and they add significant value to your SEO reports.

Another critical aspect of SEO reporting is the ability to project potential traffic gains based on improvements in search engine rankings. Although GA4 may not provide direct keyword data, you can still leverage search volume data and click-through rate (CTR) estimates to forecast the impact of ranking improvements on organic traffic. By analysing the search volume for a specific keyword and estimating the typical CTR for various ranking positions, you can calculate the potential increase in traffic that could result from moving up in the search results. This approach allows you to quantify the potential return on investment (ROI) of your SEO efforts, making it easier to justify continued investment in optimisation activities.

For instance, suppose you identify a keyword with a high search volume and estimate that moving from the third to the first position in search results could double your CTR. By applying this estimated

CTR to the search volume, you can project the additional traffic your site might receive as a result of the ranking improvement. This type of projection is invaluable for setting realistic goals and expectations with stakeholders, as it provides a clear link between your SEO efforts and potential business outcomes. Moreover, it allows you to prioritise your optimisation efforts, focusing on keywords and content that offer the greatest potential for traffic growth.

To maximise the effectiveness of your SEO reports, it is essential to present the data in a way that is both comprehensive and accessible to your audience. This means not only including detailed metrics and analysis but also contextualising the data to highlight the impact of your efforts. For example, rather than simply reporting on changes in visibility or Share of Voice, you should explain how these changes relate to your overall SEO strategy and what actions can be taken to further improve performance. Additionally, consider using visualisations such as charts and graphs to make complex data more digestible. A well-structured report that clearly communicates the value of your SEO efforts will not only inform stakeholders but also build confidence in the long-term success of your strategy.

Furthermore, it is important to recognise that SEO reporting is not just about looking backward at past performance but also about planning for the future. Regularly reviewing and updating your reports based on the latest data and trends ensures that your SEO strategy remains agile and responsive to changes in the digital landscape. This ongoing process of analysis and adjustment is key to maintaining and improving your site's performance in search results, especially in a competitive environment where search engine algorithms and user behaviours are constantly evolving.

In the context of GA4, this might mean continuously refining how you track and report on user engagement metrics, experimenting with different event tracking setups, or exploring new ways to infer keyword performance based on content interaction. With GSC, it could involve setting up alerts for significant changes in impressions or CTRs, allowing you to quickly respond to shifts in search behaviour. And with tools like SEMrush, it might involve monitoring competitors' activities more closely, identifying emerging trends, and adjusting your strategy accordingly.

Reporting on SEO efforts in the modern digital landscape requires a multifaceted approach that draws on a variety of data sources and metrics. While the transition to Google Analytics 4 has introduced new challenges, it also presents opportunities to adopt more sophisticated reporting techniques that focus on user engagement and behaviour. By integrating Google Search Console data into your reports, you can maintain a strong understanding of keyword performance and continue to refine your SEO strategy. Third-party tools like SEMrush add another layer of insight, providing visibility and competitive metrics that enhance the depth and breadth of your reporting. Finally, by projecting potential traffic gains based on search volumes and ranking improvements, you can offer stakeholders a clear and quantifiable picture of the value your SEO efforts are delivering. This comprehensive approach to SEO reporting not only ensures that your efforts are recognised but also provides the insights needed to drive ongoing success in a rapidly changing digital environment.

In today's complex SEO environment, it is no longer sufficient to rely on traditional reporting methods that focus solely on basic metrics like keyword rankings or pageviews. The evolution of tools like GA4 requires a deeper, more nuanced approach that accounts for changes in how data is collected and analysed. This means placing greater emphasis on user engagement metrics, understanding the broader context of how your content performs, and using tools like GSC and SEMrush to fill in the gaps and provide a more complete picture of your SEO performance.

The future of SEO reporting will undoubtedly continue to evolve as new technologies and methodologies emerge. However, by adopting a flexible and comprehensive approach, you can ensure that your reports remain relevant and valuable, providing the insights needed to navigate the ever-changing digital landscape. Whether you are dealing with the challenges of limited keyword data in GA4, leveraging the detailed search query data from GSC, or using advanced metrics from tools like SEMrush, the key to successful SEO reporting lies in your ability to adapt and innovate. By staying ahead of the curve and continuously refining your reporting processes, you can maintain a competitive edge and demonstrate the ongoing value of your SEO efforts in driving business success.

CHAPTER 20
THE FUTURE OF SEO, SIMPLIFIED

The SEO landscape is increasingly complex and competitive, driven by advanced search engine algorithms and evolving user behaviour. As Google and other search engines frequently update their ranking factors, and as users increasingly rely on mobile devices, voice search, and visual search technologies, a static, one-time SEO audit is no longer sufficient.

To stay competitive, businesses need a comprehensive and adaptable SEO strategy that evolves with the digital landscape. By adopting this approach, your website will remain visible, engaging, and capable of driving sustainable organic growth. An ongoing, dynamic SEO strategy is essential to achieve long-term success.

The digital marketing and SEO landscape has undergone significant changes in recent years. Traditional measures of success, like attribution and click-through rates, are increasingly challenged as major platforms like LinkedIn, Twitter, Facebook, and Instagram focus on retaining users within their ecosystems. These platforms often prioritise native content over outbound links, reducing the effectiveness of traditional click-through strategies.

Compounding these challenges, attribution has become more difficult due to privacy laws, ad blockers, and the growing use of multiple devices. With the decline of third-party cookies and stricter data protection regulations, traditional attribution models are becoming obsolete. The focus is shifting toward understanding where and how your audience is influenced rather than direct attribution.

Effective marketing strategies now require identifying the social networks, websites, podcasts, and other platforms where your target audience spends time. Optimising for these sources of influence can lead to more meaningful engagement and better results.

Artificial intelligence (AI) and machine learning are transforming SEO. AI-powered search engines like ChatGPT are changing how users interact with search engines, moving away from keyword-based queries to more conversational and contextually relevant searches. This shift necessitates new SEO strategies that focus on natural language processing (NLP) and the contextual relevance of content.

In this new landscape, high-quality, authoritative content that provides comprehensive answers will be prioritised. Google's EEAT (Experience, Expertise, Authoritativeness, Trustworthiness) principles remain crucial, but the focus will extend beyond just ranking on search engine results pages to becoming a trusted source of information for AI-driven systems.

Metrics for measuring SEO success are also evolving. Traditional metrics like page views, bounce rates, and SERP rankings are becoming less significant. New metrics, including response accuracy, engagement rate, and content utilisation, are emerging to gauge success in an AI-centric environment. These metrics measure how effectively AI models use your content to generate responses and how well users interact with AI-driven systems.

Transitioning from traditional SEO to AI-optimised content requires significant changes in strategy and skill sets. Content creators must focus on producing high-quality, authoritative content optimised for NLP, ensuring it is easily interpretable by AI models. Despite AI's capabilities, human expertise remains indispensable, as AI models require oversight to ensure accuracy and ethical use. Collaboration between content creators, editors, and subject matter experts with AI will be essential to producing reliable, high-quality content.

As the SEO landscape evolves, continuous learning and skill development in AI, NLP, and data analytics will be vital. Educational institutions and professional organisations must adapt their curricula to prepare the next generation of SEO experts for an AI-driven world. Professionals must adopt a mindset of continuous learning and be ready to pivot strategies as new technologies and methodologies emerge.

The potential rise of AI-powered search engines as primary tools for information retrieval heralds a new era for SEO. While traditional search engines may decline, the core principles of providing valuable, high-quality content will endure. By understanding and adapting to the changes brought about by AI, businesses and content creators can thrive. The collaboration between human expertise and AI will shape the future of information retrieval, ensuring businesses remain competitive in the age of AI.

The rise of zero-click searches presents another challenge for SEO professionals. A significant percentage of searches now result in no clicks, as users find the information they need directly on the search results page. This trend is driven by features like Google's Knowledge Graph, featured snippets, and AI-generated answers that provide instant information without requiring users to click through to a website.

To succeed in this environment, SEO strategies must focus on optimising for zero-click features. This involves creating content that answers users' questions concisely and effectively, ensuring it is featured prominently in search results. Structured data and schema markup are crucial for helping search engines understand and present your content in the most relevant way.

Local SEO is becoming increasingly important as users continue to rely on mobile devices and voice search for local information. Optimising for location-based queries, maintaining accurate and consistent business information across online platforms, and encouraging positive customer reviews are essential strategies. Tools like Google Business Profile and other local listing services will be vital for enhancing local SEO performance.

Voice search is revolutionising user interaction with search engines, requiring different optimisation strategies compared to traditional text-based SEO. Utilising natural language keywords, aiming for featured snippets, and focusing on local SEO are crucial for success in this area.

The rise of connected devices and the Internet of Things (IoT) is another trend influencing SEO. As more devices become connected, the way users search for and consume information will change. SEO strategies must adapt to these new behaviours, ensuring content is accessible and relevant across a range of devices and platforms.

Augmented Reality (AR) and Virtual Reality (VR) technologies are also poised to impact the future of SEO. These technologies offer new opportunities for engaging users through immersive experiences. Optimising content for AR and VR involves creating interactive and visually appealing experiences that can capture user attention and enhance engagement. By leveraging these immersive technologies, businesses can create memorable experiences that attract users and encourage them to spend more time on their site, improving overall engagement metrics.

As the digital landscape becomes more complex, the need for a comprehensive and adaptive SEO strategy becomes critical. The rise of AI and machine learning will continue to shape the future of SEO, requiring businesses to stay ahead of the curve by focusing on NLP and contextual relevance. The future of SEO lies in the seamless integration of technology and human ingenuity, creating a dynamic and adaptive approach to digital marketing that ensures long-term success.

CONCLUSION: EMBRACE THE EVER-EVOLVING WORLD OF SEO

As we conclude "Hiding Dead Bodies", it's essential to reflect on the journey we've taken together. This guide has navigated through the intricate and multifaceted world of SEO, from understanding the foundational principles to exploring advanced strategies and emerging trends. The ever-evolving nature of SEO requires constant learning, adaptation, and a willingness to innovate.

SEO is not a one-time effort but an ongoing process that demands attention to detail, strategic thinking, and a deep understanding of both your audience and the digital landscape. The insights shared in this book aim to equip you with the knowledge and tools necessary to excel in this dynamic field.

We've explored the importance of technical SEO, including website architecture, speed, and performance optimisation. These elements ensure that your website is not only accessible to search engines but also provides a seamless user experience. The significance of security, with a focus on HTTPS and safe browsing, underscores the need to protect your website and its visitors from potential threats.

Content strategy has been a central theme, emphasising the shift from outdated content marketing to a more holistic approach that values quality, relevance, and user engagement. We delved into keyword research, highlighting the balance between topic-focused content and the strategic use of keywords to capture intent-based searches. Writing for SEO and readability remains crucial, as does understanding user intent and behaviour.

The journey through off-page SEO and local strategies showcased the power of link building, social media integration, and local SEO efforts. These strategies amplify your reach, enhance your online presence, and foster community engagement.

In the realm of analytics and emerging trends, we discussed the importance of utilising tools like Google Analytics, SEMrush, and Ahrefs to track performance and refine strategies. The future of SEO will undoubtedly be influenced by AI, voice search, and new technologies such as AR and VR, which will shape how users interact with content.

Ethical SEO practices and regulatory compliance are paramount, ensuring that your efforts align with legal standards and contribute to a fair and trustworthy digital environment. Understanding and recovering from algorithm penalties, as well as conducting competitive analysis, further strengthen your SEO strategy.

As we look to the future, it's clear that the landscape of SEO will continue to evolve. Embracing change, staying informed about the latest developments, and maintaining a user-centric approach will be key to your success. The integration of AI, machine learning, and advanced analytics will offer new opportunities and challenges, pushing the boundaries of what is possible in SEO.

As SEO becomes more complex, the use of automation tools will become increasingly important. AI-powered tools that can automate keyword research, content optimisation, and even aspects of link building will be more prevalent. However, the human element—critical thinking, creativity, and strategy—will remain indispensable, as automation can only enhance, not replace, the nuanced work that SEO requires

To the readers, thank you for embarking on this journey with me. If you got this far, then your commitment to understanding and mastering SEO is commendable. Remember, the principles and strategies outlined in this guide are tools to help you navigate the digital landscape, but the true measure of success lies in your ability to adapt, innovate, and continuously strive for excellence.

Stay curious, stay informed, and most importantly, stay dedicated to providing value to your audience. The future of SEO is bright, and with the right approach, you can achieve remarkable results.

Thank you for your time, your attention, and your passion for SEO.

Here's to your continued success in the ever-evolving world of search engine optimisation.

Have fun.

SPECIAL THANKS

Christine Connolly: For everything you do for Caden.

also

Graham Carroll and Dave Jackson (Friday Agency): For teaching me more about Digital Strategy and UX than I ever knew. I thought I almost knew it all. I didn't.

Richie Lawton: For putting up with me every workday for years. Every workday. Just imagine that.

Colin and Kev: For the friendship and laughs.

John Casey: For the friendship and agency banter.

AUTHOR BIO

With over two decades of experience in digital marketing, Gavin Duff has established himself as a leading expert in the field. His extensive hands-on experience spans digital strategy, paid media, search marketing, analytics, content strategy, social media, and e-commerce across a wide array of industries.

Throughout his career, he has defined and executed highly effective PPC, SEO, display advertising, content creation, e-commerce strategies, conversion optimisation, and overall digital direction for numerous significant businesses within a client portfolio including international high-profile names.

Beyond his professional achievements, Gavin has a deep interest and qualifications in neuromarketing and cyberpsychology, particularly in understanding how humans interact with technology and advertising. This passion has driven his innovative approach to digital marketing, blending traditional techniques with cutting-edge psychological insights. He is also a member of The Psychological Society of Ireland.

In addition to his work with clients, he has shared his knowledge as a conference speaker, lecturer at Trinity College Dublin and other institutions, podcast guest, media contributor, and guest blogger. His insights have helped shape the strategies of countless businesses and have earned him a reputation as a thought leader in the digital marketing space.

www.ingramcontent.com/pod-product-compliance
Lightning Source LLC
Chambersburg PA
CBHW071159210326
41597CB00016B/1597